"Blessed is he that reac
this prophecy, and ke
therein: for the time is at nana."

MW01291856

The Revelation of Jesus Christ 1:3
The Last Book of the Bible

This book is dedicated to Larry King formerly of CNN and others who desire to know how it's all going to end and have eternal life. I initially wrote this book in 2007, after watching Barbara Walters interview Larry King on his 50th year in broadcasting. Ms. Walters asked Mr. King if he could have two things what would he wish? Mr. King said what he wished he could not have. He told Miss Walters he wished he could know how it was all going to end, and his second wish would be to have eternal life. His answers touched me. I relayed them to my 95-year-old pastor who said, "So, tell him! It's his Jewish right to know!" The Bible was written by Jewish men inspired by "the God of Israel," who wrote how it's all going to end and how to have the resurrection to eternal life (Daniel 12:1-4). Eternal life "is to the Jew first" and is free to those who believe the report of their prophets regarding the mediator of their New Covenant that God made with Israel by their Messiah.

I dedicate this book to Larry King of CNN and all others who desire to know how it's all going to end and have eternal life. The book also honors the Jewish people who have suffered much in human history beginning with their enslavement in Africa (Ps 106:22). They were chosen of God to bring His Word into the earth by way of their scribes and prophets to inform the world how it's all going to end so that people could have eternal life and govern themselves to His glory in this world. Jews were also chosen to bring forth the Savior of the World to rescue humanity from self-destruction and according to the prophet Daniel Israel's Messiah would be cut off and their Temple on the Temple Mount would be destroyed after His visitation (Daniel 9:26). Israel's Messiah was cut off and now sits at the right hand of God until His Father sends Him back to rescue the nation of Israel from annihilation during the battle of Armageddon (Daniel 7:13-14). The compilation of these prophecies were penned by Jewish prophets in Holy Scripture and like Daniel it pains me as I see their fulfillment approaching on the world's horizon, as the king of the west takes his place in the seat of power to make his nation "very great" (Daniel 7:15, 28; 8:27).

Table of Contents

Trump the King of the West at the Time of the End

The world is uneasy with the United States' election of Donald J. Trump as its forty-fifth president. One could not help but marvel at his ascendency to the presidency after publicly breaking every norm and social mores that polite society holds dear. The name "Donald" means world ruler, and no he is *not* the antichrist, but he is a man of *destiny*. Open a King James Bible and read Daniel chapter 8 with a dictionary and you cannot help but see that he is the prophesied "rough" king of the west who "at the time of the end" will fulfill the prophecy in making his nation "very great." (Daniel 8:9) Televangelists fail to inform their audiences of this prophecy that once served to predict the rise of Alexander the Great, the mighty western Grecian king that would conquer the Mideast; that no one could withstand as he put Europe on the map as a force to be reckoned with. The prophecy states of itself that it will again serve "at the time of the end" to identify a king of the west with the disposition of a *"rough goat"* that no nation will be able to withstand as he makes his nation "very great" prior to an unthinkable event that will occur that will cause four nations to vie as superpowers. "In the latter times of their kingdom," one will arise who Daniel identifies as "the little horn" known to Christians as antichrist (Daniel 8:9).

The prophet Daniel famous for interpreting "the handwriting on the wall" in Iraq (Babylon) is the same Daniel of the lion's den who wrote of a prophetic vision that was for an "appointed time" - "the time of the end." He had this vision in front of a river in Iraq. His dual purposed vision points out that in the end times a "rough" leader of the west, whom he identifies as a king with the character of a Billy goat will be known for his stubborn personality. The prophet wrote of this king of the west calling him in parable a "he goat" who will be moved with "choler." Webster's defines *choler* as *"a ready disposition to irritation. 2) Irascible marked by a hot temper and easily provoked to anger."* Oxford's Dictionary defines being moved with "choler" as *"a peevish temperament easily provoked to anger."* Daniel forecast that "at the time of the end" this king of the west will "be moved with choler" as his ire is stirred against *Persia* that has been called Iran since 1936 (Daniel 8:5). The first portion of Daniel 8 is in parable form describing the western leader launching an air attack as a "he goat" whose "feet touched not the ground" as it tackles a "ram having two horns." Later, in the chapter describing Daniel's parable it reveals that the "two horns" are the kings of Media and Persia/Iran. Daniel prophesied that "at the time of the end" a "rough goat" like king from the west will trample the leaders of Iraq and Iran into the dust. On September 11, 2001, a king of the west was caught flat-footed when he was reading a children's book, ironically titled, *"My Pet Goat"* to school kids in Florida, when his nation was air attacked. Later, this western leader, President George W. Bush under his motto "Stay the course" initiated an unprovoked attack on Iraq in a war called "Iraqi Freedom" leading to its dictator (i.e. king according to Daniel) Saddam Hussein being toppled in death in 2003. This was the first stage of this prophecy's fulfillment of having the first horn crushed by Hussein's death.

Presently, in 2017, this war still endures, because Daniel predicted that the same attack near the territory of Media conquered by Alexander must also topple Iran's\Persia's leader. However, when this *"rough goat"* leader from the west defeats Persia (Iran), Daniel writes that his nation will become *"very great"* (Daniel 8:8). At this time, God has positioned in the West's seat of power a man whose name Donald means "world ruler" as "the king of the west" in these end times and has established him with a goat's stubbornness that has served him well in ascending to highest executive office in the United States under his motto to "Make America Great Again". Thus, President Trump is a man of destiny as he ignites the fuse in the Mideast in "the time of the end" as he strives to make his nation "very great".

As the world reels in amazement at the election of Donald Trump, Daniel wrote regarding the kings of nations that he prophesied about and dealt with stating that it was *"to the intent that the living may know that the most High ruleth in the kingdoms of men, and giveth it to whomsoever he will...."* (Daniel 4:17) On January 20, 2017, God gave the scepter of American rulership to Donald J. Trump as the West's president "for such a time as this – the time of the end." (Esther 4:14; Daniel 8:17) He is the king from the West who Daniel wrote of that will appear in the last days to attack Iran and make his nation "very great" (Daniel 8:8).

This book is to alert the world's biblically illiterate public about Jewish prophecy regarding the times in which we live. Prophecies once heard in church are now seen on television and the public-at-large do not realize they are witnessing the fulfillment of Bible prophecies counting down to the Second Coming of Jesus Christ. He was prophesied to come first as Israel's rejected suffering Messiah as *Messiah Ben Joseph*, the name of his stepfather the Virgin Mary's husband. He is prophesied to return, in the last days, as the kingly son of David called *Messiah Ben David*. (*Ben* in Jewish culture means son of) as shown in His lineage in Matthew 1).

Though the intelligentsia of the West relegates Jesus' Second Coming and the Bible as mythology, God instructed *"Daniel to shut up the words, and seal the book [of Daniel], until the time of the end: when many shall run to and fro and knowledge shall be increased."* (Daniel 12:4) On January 20, 2017, a bewildered world watched in amazement as this "rough" western leader was inaugurated and now is seated on earth's most powerful throne in the West with the predicted temperament forecasted in the book of Daniel. Thus, it is now "the time of the end" as God's clock begins to tick down to the end of time. Understand that when the Bible uses such phraseology as the "end of days" or "the last days" or "the time of the end," this does not indicate a doomsday scenario. It simply means it will be the last days prior to Israel's Messiah's return to earth to rule and reign as king of the world in a new administration of righteousness that the world has never experienced with Israel elevated to the head of the nations. Thus, Jesus told His chosen Jewish people that, "When you see these things begin to come to pass, then look up, and lift up your heads; for your redemption draweth nigh." (Luke 21:28)

This millennial age opened with airwaves and newspapers filled with shocking headlined events. Weather has become so tumultuous that it seems commonplace to hear of flooding, scores of tornadoes touching down in an evening, tsunami threats, cyclones, and fierce hurricanes destroying coastal regions, and global record setting temperatures. The political climate is such that small nations are defying superpowers by launching and detonating nuclear weapons against stern warnings. First world nations are now threatened by the seepage of nuclear arms into the hands of terrorists.

This new millennium has witnessed the atomic scientists' Doomsday's Clock in 2017 inch from three minutes to two minutes and thirty seconds toward the midnight; the midnight of humanity's catastrophic destruction in their mind. At the advent of the new millennium in 2001, the United States of America experienced her first traumatic Mid-East based terrorist attack, for her alliance with the nation of Israel. Afterwards, a United States president responded with an unprovoked attack on Iraq then later honestly admitted its basis for such a war proved groundless. The Middle East has become the epicenter of international turmoil with Israel's very existence being openly threatened by certain Arab states, which perplexes world leaders.

Israel always had enemies but with increasing frequency, terrorism toward Israelis by suicide bombers in the name of God turned peaceful shopping trips, wedding days, and ordinary bus rides in Israel into sights of unspeakable carnage.

This generation has seen blazed across the New York Times and heard over CNN airwaves of asteroids heading toward planet earth and a small one landed in Russia. Is all this coincidental? No. Thousands of years ago, Jewish prophets recorded all these events, and more, would converge in the generation that would see Israel become a nation; which occurred in May 1948. The prophecies once heard in church are now seen on television, the west's war with and defeat of Iraq's leader and its soon defeat of Iran's leader was predicted thousands of years before Christ by the prophet Daniel.

It is the fourth quarter and the two-minute warning is about to sound on the field of play. With the use of Jewish prophecies as a checklist, this book is a barometer of world events and conditions as it counts down to the end of this age, as we know it. This book is a compilation of Jewish prophecies from the ancient texts from old and new testaments. Most Americans have ignored and neglected their bibles that prophetic events are being fulfilled before their eyes and they do not even recognize them. This book serves only as a checklist of the ancient Jewish prophecies for you to note them as they occur.

This is *not* a menu of the order of their execution as they come to pass. Again President Donald Trump is <u>not</u> the antichrist, but it is interesting that his name means "world ruler". "And who knoweth that thou (Donald Trump) has come to the kingdom for such a time as this." (Esther 4:14) Therefore, as the Scripture has stated, let us pray "**for kings, and for all that are in authority; that we may lead a quiet and peaceable life in all godliness and honesty**." (1 Timothy 2:2) Godspeed, Mr. President. Our prayers are with you.

Section One: Signs of the Last Days

✓ "The Beginning of Sorrows"

Ground Zero: Israel to Become a Nation

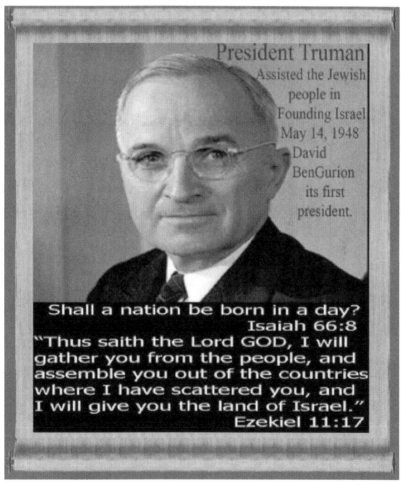

President Truman Assisted the Jewish people in Founding Israel May 14, 1948 David BenGurion its first president.

Shall a nation be born in a day?
Isaiah 66:8
"Thus saith the Lord GOD, I will gather you from the people, and assemble you out of the countries where I have scattered you, and I will give you the land of Israel."
Ezekiel 11:17

"Thus saith the Lord GOD; I will even gather you from the people, and assemble you out of the countries where ye have been scattered, **and I will give you the land of Israel.**" (The Prophet Ezekiel 11:17)

"But, the LORD liveth, that brought up the children of Israel from the land of the north, and from all the lands whither he had driven them: **and I will bring them again into their land that I gave unto their fathers.**" (The Prophet Jeremiah 16:15)

"And I will return the captivity of my people Israel, and they shall build the waste cities and inhabit them; and they shall plant vineyards and drink the wine thereof; they also shall make gardens and eat the fruit of them. **and I will plant them upon their land and they shall no more be pulled up out of their land which I have given them, says the Lord thy God.**" (The Prophet Amos 9:14-15)

"Who hath heard such a thing? who hath seen such things? Shall the earth be made to bring forth in one day? or shall a **nation** be **born** at once? for as soon as Zion travailed, she brought forth her children." (Isaiah 66:8)

✓ This prophecy was fulfilled May 14, 1948

✓ WW II was the birth pangs of travail that brought about the nation of Israel.

Prophecy No. 1
Terrorism Towards Israel Predicted

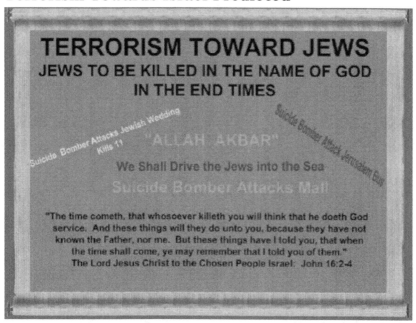

The Apostle Paul wrote, "Know this that in the last days perilous times shall come." Jesus prophesied to the Jewish people in Israel that, "The time cometh, that whosoever killeth you will think that he doeth God service." (1 Timothy 3:1-2, John 16:2)

✓ Suicide Bombings in Israel in The Name of God

✓ 2015 Killing of Jews in France because of magazine cartoon

More Terror Attacks in God's name to Come

Prophecy No. 2

Great Earthquakes & Pandemics, and Fearful Sights

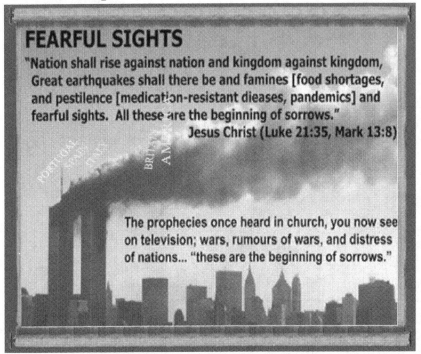

FEARFUL SIGHTS

"Nation shall rise against nation and kingdom against kingdom, Great earthquakes shall there be and famines [food shortages, and pestilence [medication-resistant dieases, pandemics] and fearful sights. All these are the beginning of sorrows."

Jesus Christ (Luke 21:35, Mark 13:8)

The prophecies once heard in church, you now see on television; wars, rumours of wars, and distress of nations... "these are the beginning of sorrows."

Fearful sights = World Trade Center toppling, School shootings, Boston Marathon Bombing, and terror attacks in Spain, England, and France, and Mideast beheadings of Christians. More fearful sights to come.

"Great earthquakes shall be in divers places, and famines, and pestilences [pandemic diseases]; and fearful sights." - Jesus Christ (Luke 21:11)

Great Earthquakes in diverse places:
Japan 2011 18,000 dead. Haiti 2010 316,000 dead.
China 2008 90,000 dead. Pakistan 2005 80,000 dead
Indonesia 2004 230,000 dead. More to come.

"All these are the beginning of sorrows." (Matthew 24:8)
More great earthquakes to come.

Famines = Ethiopia & Sudan: More food shortages to come. Water shortage in 2015, and more water shortages to come due to climate change. Al Roker of the NBC Today Show stated in 2014 that Americans will soon be fighting one another over water resources in the not to distant future.

Pestilence/Pandemics: The 2014 Ebola outbreak that threatened the world. The 2016 Zika virus. The Center of Disease Control fears more pandemics

Prophecy No. 3
Fierce Seas Producing Unprecedented Hurricanes

FIERCE HURRICANES, TIDAL WAVES, & TSUNAMIS

"There shall be signs in the sun, moon, and stars; and on earth distress of nations, the seas and the waves thereof roaring [hurricanes, tsunamis, tidal waves]." Luke 21:25

"And there shall be signs in the sun, and in the moon, and in the stars; and upon the earth distress of nations, with perplexity; the sea and the waves roaring [fierce hurricanes, tidal waves and tsunamis]." (Luke 21:25)

Weather is the earth's way of cooling itself, and with the rise of global temperatures, the earth's weather will become increasingly more violent as it attempts to cool itself, spawning horrendous hurricanes, treacherous tornadoes, and dramatic flooding.

✓ 2012 Super storm Sandy hit New Jersey Shore
✓ 2005 Hurricane Katrina
✓ 2004 Thailand Tsunami
✓ 2004 Three Florida Hurricanes in one year
  More fierce hurricanes to come

"This generation shall not pass away until all these things are fulfilled. Truly I say unto you, when ye shall see all these things, know that it is near, even at the doors. And except those days be shortened there would be no flesh spared alive upon the earth. But for the elect's sake they shall be shortened." Jesus Christ (St. Matthew 24:21-22)

See the "Best Prophecy Video Ever"
www.youtube.com/watch?v=JxEvBw-GbjI

From author's webstite www.ProphecyChecklist.com

Signs in the Sun and in the Moon

There shall be signs in the sun and in the moon"
America's coast to coast eclipse in 2017 with the sun and moon.

Massive sunspots emitted enormous solar flares in 2017

"The sun shall be turned into darkness, and the moon into blood, before the great and terrible day of the LORD come." (Joel 2:31)

"I will cover the heaven, and make the stars thereof dark; I will cover the sun with a cloud, and the moon shall not give her light." (Ezek. 32:7)

More signs in the heavens to come...

Prophecy No. 4
Information Age Prophesied

"<u>At the time of the end</u>, many shall run to and fro and knowledge shall be increased." (The Prophet Daniel 12:4)

✓ Invention of the Automobile & Aerospace travel

✓ Cloning & Biotechnology and other medical advances

✓ Information Superhighway & Computer age

Prophecy No. 5
Unprecedented Greed: The Rich Fraudulently Withholding Wages From Laborers in the End Times

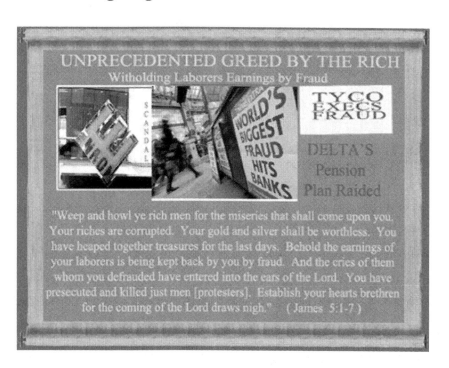

UNPRECEDENTED GREED BY THE RICH
Witholding Laborers Earnings by Fraud

WORLD'S BIGGEST FRAUD HITS BANKS

SCANDAL

TYCO EXECS FRAUD

DELTA'S Pension Plan Raided

"Weep and howl ye rich men for the miseries that shall come upon you. Your riches are corrupted. Your gold and silver shall be worthless. You have heaped together treasures for the last days. Behold the earnings of your laborers is being kept back by you by fraud. And the cries of them whom you defrauded have entered into the ears of the Lord. You have presecuted and killed just men [protesters]. Establish your hearts brethren for the coming of the Lord draws nigh." (James 5:1-7)

"Go now, ye rich men, weep and howl for your miseries that shall come upon you. Your riches are corrupted... Ye have heaped treasure together for the last days. Behold, the hire [money] of the laborers who have reaped down your fields, which is of you kept back by fraud, crieth: and the cries of them which have reaped are entered into the ears of the Lord... Ye have lived in pleasure on the earth, and been wanton; ye have nourished your hearts, as in a day of slaughter. Ye have condemned and killed the just [protesters]; and he doth not resist you. ⬜Be patient therefore, brethren, unto the coming of the Lord... Be ye also patient; establish your hearts: for the coming of the Lord draweth nigh."
(James 5:1-8)

"Evil men and seducers shall wax worse and worse deceiving and being deceived." (2 Timothy 3:13)

✓   Junk Bond Scandal   ✓ Saving and Loan Scandal

✓   Kenneth Lay of Enron   ✓ Retirements Raided by Fraud

✓   Bernie Ebbers WorldCom ✓ Dennis Kozlowski of Tyco

✓   John Rigas of Adelphia   ✓ Stephen Hilbert of Conseco

✓   AIG insufficient mortgage backed securities

✓   Bernie Madoff of Maddoff Investment Securities

✓   Bear Stearns Bankruptcy   ✓ Merrill Lynch Bankruptcy

✓   Lehman Brothers Bankruptcy   ✓ Nations bankrupted

More catastrophic economic fallout to come...

Prophecy No. 6
Successful Gay Rights Movement Predicted

Internationally Successful Gay Rights Movement

GAY PRIDE

"As it was in the days of Lot [who lived in the legendary city of Sodom], thus shall it be when the son of man is revealed [at His 2nd Coming]."
Jesus Christ - Luke 17:27-30, Genesis chapter 19

"For as the lightning, that lighteneth out of the one part under heaven, shineth unto the other part under heaven; so shall also the Son of man be in his day....And as it was in the days of Noah [violence covered the earth and great floods worldwide do to the ancient climate change of his day], so shall it be also in the days of the Son of man... Likewise also as it was in the days of Lot...even thus shall it be in the day when the Son of man is revealed." (Luke 17:24-30)

✓ ☐Jesus stated that at His coming life will be not only as it was during the days of Noah but also as it was "in the days of Lot." (Luke 17:28) "Remember Lot's wife." (Luke 17:32) Both Lot and his wife lived in Sodom, a city legendarily famous for its acceptance of the homosexual lifestyle from "the old to the young" (Genesis 19:4). Sodom had degenerated to the point where men were gang-raping men during Abraham's time. (Genesis 19:5, 8) Thus, Christ prophesied of a successful gay rights movement, "as it was in the days of Lot," that will encompass the globe prior to His Second Coming. (Jesus Christ –Luke 17:28-30, the story of Lot in Sodom is found in Genesis 19)

✓ ☐In 2015, the United States Supreme Court recognized same sex marriage in America. The gay rights movement is not exclusively a sign for America but is occurring worldwide.

✓ ☐According to Genesis 19:14, when Lot tried to warn the inhabitants of Sodom of God's impending judgment, they thought he was mocking (joking), so shall it be for believers who attempt to warn the world of God's approaching judgment called the Tribulation Period also known as "the time of Jacob's [Israel's] trouble."(Jeremiah 30:7)

Prophecy No. 7

Jerusalem Become a Burden Around to Her Allies

"Behold, I will make Jerusalem a cup of trembling unto all the people round about ... **And in that day will I make Jerusalem a burdensome stone for all people: all that burden themselves with it shall be cut in pieces,** though all the people of the earth be gathered together against it." (The Prophet Zechariah 12:2-3)

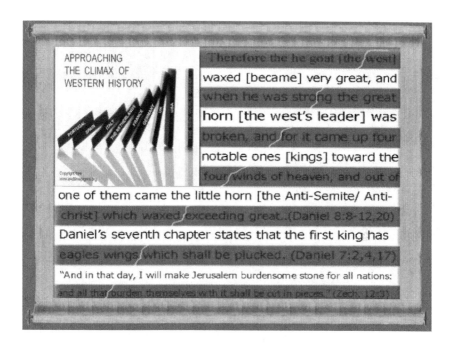

✓ The United States remains loyally allied with Israel

✓ Terrorist attack on American soil

✓ President Trump wants to move U.S. Embassy to Jerusalem.

Prophecy No. 8

Gospel of the Kingdom is Spread Throughout World

"And this gospel of the kingdom shall be preached in all the world for a witness unto all nations; and then shall the end come." (Matthew 24:14)

✓ "Passion of the Christ" is available in every language.

✓ South Korean Churches lead world in sending evangelists.

Prophecy No. 9

2nd Coming Mocked as Ridiculous in the Last Days

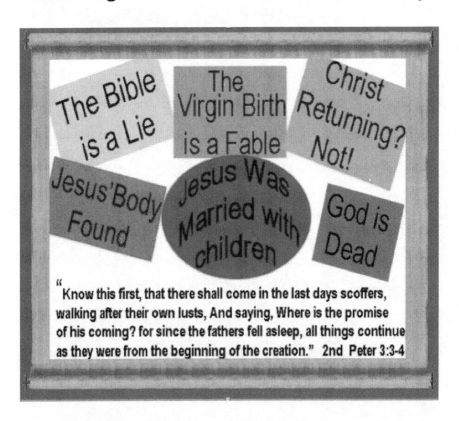

The Bible is a Lie

The Virgin Birth is a Fable

Christ Returning? Not!

Jesus' Body Found

Jesus Was Married with children

God is Dead

" Know this first, that there shall come in the last days scoffers, walking after their own lusts, And saying, Where is the promise of his coming? for since the fathers fell asleep, all things continue as they were from the beginning of the creation." 2nd Peter 3:3-4

"Knowing this first, **that there shall come in the last days scoffers,** walking after their own lusts, and saying, Where is the promise of his coming? for since the fathers [Jewish fathers: *Abraham, Isaac, and Jacob*] fell asleep [died], all things continue as they were from the beginning of the creation." (2 Peter 3:3-4)

"Enoch also, the seventh from Adam, prophesied of these, saying, Behold, the Lord cometh with ten thousands of his saints, **To execute judgment upon all, and to convince all that are ungodly among them of all their ungodly deeds which they have ungodly committed, and of all their hard speeches which ungodly sinners have spoken against him.**" (Jude 14-15)

✓ False claims such as Jesus bones found recently

✓ False claim Jesus was married to Mary Magdalene

✓ The Da Vinci Code, The Last Temptation of Christ, and Jesus Christ Superstar making a mockery the Messiah

✓ Popular comedians mock Jesus Christ, His message, the Rapture known as "the blessed hope," and His 2nd Coming

✓ Atheist encouraging people to mock the Second Coming

More hard speeches against Christ prior to His return come

Section Two: The West to War With the Leaders of Iraq (Media) and Iran (Persia) as Prophesied by Daniel

Iran and Iraq were once part of the Medo-Persian Empire. As a child, Daniel was kidnapped and taken to Babylon in ancient Persia's province now called Iraq. There he interpreted "the handwriting on the wall" and wrote the following prophecy regarding what would befall Iraq and Iran in the last days. Daniel describes, in precise detail, how "at the time of the end," *a king of Media* [Iraq], described as one of two horns on a ram, would engage in expanding his territory "pushing westward, and northward, and southward," so that no one could withstand him and he would become great. (Daniel 8:4)

Saddam Hussein proved to be that leader who enlarged his Iraqi kingdom into Kuwait and posed a threat to Saudi Arabia. This occurred in the early 90's and it stirred the ire of then U.S. President George Herbert Walker Bush. President Bush (41) did not fulfill Daniel's prophecy because Saddam

Hussein was not killed in his attack. (Daniel 8:5, 21) Daniel's prophecy specifically stated that "at the time of the end" a ruler from the West, who Daniel depicts as a stubborn male goat, will be "moved with choler" and initiate an unprovoked attack on this Mideast king and stomp him to death as a first step (Daniel 8:7-20).

It is noteworthy that the king from the west will war against the kings of Media and Persia [Iraq and Iran] not their people. The fulfillment of this prophecy was by President George W. Bush (43) thus indicating that the office of U.S. presidency "at the time of the end" represents the king from the west. According to Daniel's prophecy, after the king from the west destroys this particular Mideast king, the West's king will also destroy the second horn symbolizing the king of Persia (Iran), and stomp its leader to death. Scripture points out that no nation will be able deliver either king out of this western ruler's hand. Daniel refers to him, as a rough he-goat that defeats the two kings, Iraq and Iran respectively, then he informs us that his western ruler's nation will "wax [become] very great," and in the midst of its greatness its power [horns represent power in Scripture] "shall be broken."(Dan. 8:8) Afterwards, four nations will arise to fill the vacuum of world leadership. Daniel then foretell of the rise of the Antichrist that he depicts as "the *little horn*." (Dan. 8:9, 7:8)

As we look on the world scene, we see the stage is being set before our eyes by the unseen hand of Providence that is bringing this prophecy to pass. Major players in the last days will be Egypt, Israel, Russia, Assyria, Iraq/Iran [also called Assyria/Babylon/Media/Persia] and the kings of the East, notably China (Revelation 16:12). The following prophecy was initially fulfilled by Alexander the Great, but according to Daniel 8:17, 23 its pattern will again serve for the end times or "the time of the end." According to Daniel 8:27, this prophecy literally made the prophet sick, and it is very troubling to us who believe "the Scripture of truth." (An end time prophecy pictorial for you to share at www.prophecychecklist.com)

Daniel 8

¹In the third year of the reign of King Belshazzar a vision appeared unto me, even unto me Daniel, after that which appeared unto me at the first. ²And I saw in a vision; and it came to pass, when I saw, that I was at Shushan in the palace, which is in the province of Elam; and I saw in a vision, and I was by the river of Ulai. ³Then I lifted up mine eyes, and saw, and, behold, there stood before the river **a ram which had two horns**: and the two horns were high; but one was higher than the other, and the higher came up last. ⁴**I saw the ram pushing westward, and northward, and southward; so that no beasts might stand before him,** neither was there any that could deliver out of his hand; but he did according to his will, and became great. ⬜⁵And as I was considering, behold, an **he goat came from the west** on the face of the whole earth, and touched not the ground: and the goat had a notable horn between his eyes. ⬜⁶**And he came to the ram that had two horns, which I had seen standing before the river, and ran unto him in the fury of his power.** ⁷And I saw him come close unto the ram, and **he was moved with choler against him, and smote the ram, and brake his two horns: and there was**

no power in the ram to stand before him, but he cast him down to the ground, and stamped upon him: and there was none that could deliver the ram out of his hand. ⁸Therefore the **he goat waxed very great: and when he was strong, the great horn was broken;** and for it **came up four** notable ones **toward** the four winds of heaven. ⁹And **out of one of them** came forth **a little horn**, which waxed exceeding great, toward the south, and toward the east, and toward the pleasant land ¹⁰And it waxed great, even to the host of heaven; and it cast down some of the host and of the stars to the ground, and stamped upon them. ¹¹Yea, he magnified himself even to the prince of the host, and by him the daily sacrifice was taken away, and the place of the sanctuary was cast down. ¹²And an host was given him against the daily sacrifice by reason of transgression, and it cast down the truth to the ground; and it practiced, and prospered. ¹³Then I heard one saint speaking, and another saint said unto that certain saint which spake, How long shall be the vision concerning the daily sacrifice, and the transgression of desolation, to give both the sanctuary and the host to be trodden under foot? ¹⁴And he said unto me, Unto two thousand and three hundred days; then shall the sanctuary be cleansed. **¹⁵And it came to pass, when I, even I Daniel, had seen the vision, and sought for the meaning,** then, behold, there stood before me as the appearance of a man. ¹⁶And **I heard a man's voice between** the banks of Ulai, **which called, and said, Gabriel, make this man to understand the vision.** ¹⁷So he came near where I stood: and when he came, I was afraid, and fell upon my face: but he said unto me, Understand, O son of man: for **at the time of the end shall be the vision**. [18]Now as he was speaking with me, I was in a deep sleep on my face toward the ground: but he touched me, and set me upright. [19]And he said, Behold, **I will make thee know** what shall be in the last end of the indignation: for at the time appointed the end shall be. [20]**The ram which thou sawest having two horns are the kings of Media [Iraq] and Persia [Iran].** [21]**And the rough goat is the king of Grecia [the seat of western civilization]: and the great horn [power] that is between his eyes is the first king.** [22]Now that being broken, whereas four stood up for it, four kingdoms shall stand up out of the nation, but not in his power. ☐[23]And **in the latter time of their kingdom,** when the transgressors are come to the full, a king of fierce countenance, and understanding dark sentences, shall stand up [the Antichrist\Antimessiah]. [24]And his power shall be mighty, but not by his own power: and he shall destroy wonderfully, and shall prosper, and practice, and shall destroy the mighty and the holy people. [25]And through his policy also he shall cause craft to prosper in his hand; and he shall magnify himself in his heart, and by peace shall destroy many: he shall also stand up against the Prince of princes [Jesus Christ the Son of God]; but he shall be broken without hand. ☐[26]And the vision of the evening and the morning which was told is true: wherefore shut thou up the vision; for it shall be for many days. ☐[27]And I Daniel fainted, and was sick certain days; afterward I rose up, and did the king's business; and I was astonished at the vision, but none understood it."

Daniel 8 KJV

The Legend of Daniel's prophetic vision in our time:

Horns	=	National leaders Power
Ram's 1st Horn / King of Media (Iraq) who angers western king	=	Former leader of Iraq Saddam Hussein now buried in the dust of the earth
Ram's 2nd Horn /King of Persia (Iran)	=	Leader of Iran
He Goat's HORN (King of the West)	=	Presidency of the United States
The Little Horn, King of fierce Countenance	=	The Anti-semite Antichrist/Antimessiah
He goat's body	=	United States of America
The ram's body	=	Iraq and Iran
Gabriel	=	Archangel
Mighty & Holy People	=	Israel & Believers in Christ

While in the Persian province that encompassed Iraq and Iran, Daniel penned this ancient prophecy regarding what was to become of this region in the last days. He prophesied that the West will destabilize the Middle East by defeating the leaders of Media (Iraq) and Persia (Iran). The first part of this prophecy was fulfilled by the West's leader, George W. Bush who attacked Iraq's leader, Saddam Hussein, and as according to the prophecy, he now rests in the dust of the earth.

At the writing of this book, we are looking forward to the fulfillment of the second half of this prophecy in which the leader or *king of the west* removes Persia's (Iran's) king resulting in many years of Mid-east wars and rumors of wars. According to the prophecy, there shall be three leaders after the first king, Saddam Hussein's, violent removal by the west. Years later, his replacement will be removed in wartime not involving the west. (Daniel 11:19) The third leader will set about repairing the Persian Gulf's infrastructure and Daniel describes him as a "raiser of taxes," then a short time into his reign he will die of natural causes. (Daniel 11:20)

Afterwards, a wonderful peacemaker, who will eventually show himself as the greatest Anti-Semite ever known, will enter the world's stage with a peace plan for the Mid-East according to the prophet. (Daniel 11:21) Christians refer to this coming Mid-East peacemaker as the Antichrist. The Bible calls him "The Beast" in its last book where he appears. (See Section Six: The Anti-Semite/ Antichrist)

He's Got Your Goat
The chief characteristic of a goat is its stubborn disposition toward irritations. It is no secret that President George W. Bush, from the great state of Texas, is not one who wavers, but is a stubbornly determined man. One need only to perform an Internet search on words "George Bush" and "stubborn" to see myriads of professional articles written in regards to this former president's steadfast disposition. Throughout his presidency, President Bush uttered his motto which became the insignia of his presidency was that he was going to "Stay

the course." It is of interest that the prophet Daniel refers to this former western leader as a "he goat from the west."

It is interesting how God subtly let the world know that President George W. Bush was to fulfill the role of the "he goat" king of the west in Daniel's prophecy. On the morning of September 11, 2001 while President George W. Bush was visiting an elementary school in Florida, he was alerted that terrorists had rammed planes into the World Trade Center's twin towers in New York. This moment was captured on film for the world to see. President Bush was seated and reading a story to elementary school children.

Filmmaker Michael Moore, in his film *Fahrenheit 911*, terribly ridiculed President Bush for remaining seated for what seemed to be an inordinate amount of time with a child's book in his hand after hearing the news of the attack on America at such a crucial point that was to impact the world. The filmmaker mercilessly made President Bush out to be a spectacle; however, it was the hand of God that directed this spectacle for the whole world to see. It was at that time that God gave the world a glimpse of who President George W. Bush was to model in Daniel's prophecy. The title of the story that President Bush was reading at the time he was alerted of the attack, was *My Pet Goat*. In the aftermath of what is called 9-11, President Bush, against world opinion, stubbornly initiated war against a king whose country was near that of the Medes. That leader was Iraq's Saddam Hussein) who did not have weapons of mass destruction as thought, yet he was put to death for his crimes against humanity (Dan. 8:7, 20).

The Man Who Would Be King

In the year 2000, George W. Bush became President through one of the most controversial elections in American history. However, according to the book of Daniel, the prophet wrote, **"Blessed be the name of God for ever and ever: for wisdom and might are his: And he changeth the times and the seasons: he removeth kings, and setteth up kings ...."** (Dan. 2:20-21)   Though it may be distasteful to some people, according to these writings of the prophet, rulers
are set up by the Most High God, who rules in the kingdom of men. (Dan. 4:17) A former King of Iraq, Nebuchadnezzar, King of Babylon, decreed in the book of Daniel "that the most High ruleth in the kingdom of men, and giveth it to whomsoever he will, and [he] setteth up over it the basest of men." (Dan. 4:17)

King Solomon wrote, "The king's heart is in the hand of the LORD, as the rivers of water: he turneth it whithersoever he will." (Prov. 21:1) After destroying the king of Media, according to Daniel's prophecy, the king of western civilization will complete his attack, this time against the leader of Persia (Iran) trouncing him to the ground breaking him as the second horn. (Dan. 8:7, 20) Then, that western nation will become "very great". (Dan. 8:8)

In his attempt to establish democracy in the former Medo-Persian Gulf region, President George W. Bush, unbeknownst to himself or his cabinet members, fulfilled Bible prophecy as God's proverbial pet goat. According to Daniel's prophecy, President Bush's intention of ultimately establishing an autonomous democracy in the Gulf region will be successful.

The prophecy later reads that the actions of this western leader will eventually bring to power the Anti-Semite Antichrist who will "obtain the kingdom by flatteries," otherwise known as a democratic campaign. (Dan. 11:21, 32) It is interesting that this king of the west who will accomplish these things is not just called a goat, known for its stubborn disposition, but is called a "he goat" which means *male goat.* Unfortunately, the prophecy reads that, after the West becomes great, in the midst of its greatness the horn of its power shall be broken. Its superpower will be split among four nations as power shifts to the oil rich Mid-East and to China who will field a 200 million man army as she harnesses the armies of the "kings of the east." (Dan. 8:8, 21)

The Five "Inferior" Eras of World Superpowers

Many have seen The *Ten Commandments* epic *in which* Hebrews were enslaved in Africa, and God freed them to show the world His power to overthrow the strongest nation on earth. God planned that His chosen people would never be enslaved again. However, when His people chose to serve other gods, He, in judgment, appointed them to five eras ruled by "inferior" nations until He sends His Son back to earth at the end of the time of Gentile world rulership (Daniel 2:39; 7:13-14).

The Almighty revealed this plan in a dream to the most powerful king in Daniel's time, "Nebuchadnezzar the King of Babylon" (Iraq). Scripture calls him a *king of kings.* Daniel interpreted Nebuchadnezzar's dream of a statue of a king made of five metals from a gold head, a silver chest, a brass belly, iron legs, and ends with feet of iron mixed with clay.

Note that all metals following the golden head represented kingdoms that ranked inferior to Nebuchadnezzar's till the end of time. These eras are called "the times of the Gentiles," wherein God's Hebrew people would be under the dominion of Gentiles till "the time of the end." (Luke 21:24)

Daniel gave this King of Babylon the interpretation of the king's dream of this metal statue stating that Nebuchadnezzar is considered a "king of kings" and his reign over earth is represented as the statue's head of gold. Daniel informed Nebuchadnezzar that after him will arise four other superpower eras *inferior* to his that will rule earth. The exact passage is as follows in Daniel chapter 2.

³⁶This is the dream; and we will tell the interpretation thereof before the king. ³⁷ *Thou, O king, art a king of kings: for the God of heaven hath given thee a kingdom, power, and strength, and glory.* ³⁸ *And* wheresoever the children of men dwell, the beasts of the field and the fowls of the heaven hath he given into thine hand, and hath made thee ruler over them all [a superpower]. *Thou art this head of gold.* ³⁹ *And after thee shall arise another kingdom inferior to thee* [a replacing superpower], *and another third kingdom of brass* a replacing superpower, *which shall bear* rule over all the earth [a superpower]. ⁴⁰ *And the fourth kingdom shall be strong as iron: forasmuch as iron breaketh in pieces and subdueth all things: and as iron that breaketh all these, shall it break in pieces and bruise.* ⁴¹ *And whereas thou sawest the feet and toes, part of potters' clay, and part of iron, the kingdom shall be divided; but there shall be in it of the strength of the iron, forasmuch as thou sawest the iron mixed with miry clay.* ⁴² *And as the toes of the feet were part of iron, and part of clay, so the kingdom shall be partly strong, and partly broken.* ⁴³ *And*

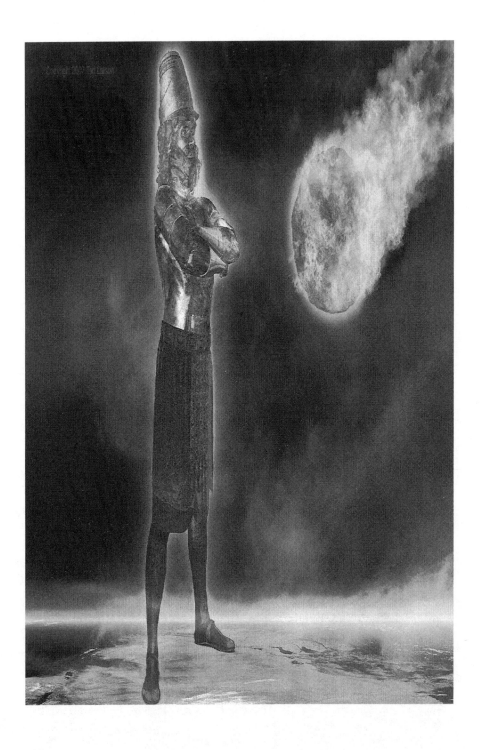

whereas thou sawest iron mixed with miry clay, they shall mingle themselves with the seed of men: but they shall not cleave one to another, even as iron is not mixed with clay.

Era's Represented on Metal Statue in Nebuchadnezzar's Dream

Head of Gold Nebuchadnezzar Babylon's world rule

Statue's *Chest and Arms* of Silver Xerxes' Persian Empire's rule

Statue's Brass *Belly to Thighs* powerful Alexander the Great's Rule

Statue's *Legs* of Iron European's Graco-Roman Rule till to the present

Feet & Toes of Iron & Clay Europeans' rule broken by 3rd world people

Permission of artist Ted Larson
http://digitalartbytedlarson.net/store
A *Rock* hits Statue's feet destroying it and grows representing Jesus Christ at His Second Coming establishing His kingdom that engulfs world rule.

⁴⁴And in the days of these kings shall the God of heaven set up a kingdom, which shall never be destroyed: and the kingdom shall not be left to other people, but it shall break in pieces and consume all these kingdoms, and it shall stand for ever. ⁴⁵Forasmuch as thou sawest that the stone was cut out of the mountain without hands, and that it brake in pieces the iron, the brass, the clay, the silver, and the gold; the great God hath made known to the king what shall come to pass hereafter: and the dream is certain, and the interpretation thereof sure. ⁴⁶ Then the king Nebuchadnezzar fell upon his face, and worshipped Daniel, and commanded that they should offer an oblation and sweet odours unto him. ⁴⁷ The king answered unto Daniel, and said, Of a truth it is, that your God is a God of gods, and a Lord of kings, and a revealer of secrets, seeing thou couldest reveal this secret."

Where are we on this Metal Statue?

Presently, we are in the longest era, symbolized by the statue's long legs of iron, as Europeans have remained superpowers of world dominance for over 2,000 years. However, "at the time of the end" Daniel describes the advent of a goat stubborn western king who will arise from the west and destroy Persia Iran) in his last act. Daniel the prophet also discloses that this western king will succeed in making his nation "very great" (Dan. 8:8). Scripture reports that when this man is strong, enjoying the fruits of his labor, a catastrophe will happen and four nations will rise and fill the void left by his nation as superpower shifts from the West to the Mid and Far East. "Kings of the east" will play an important rule in the last days according to Revelation 16:12. Unfortunately, when the West falls, it will weaken the iron grip European nations enjoyed over the last 2,000 years in which Rome by crucifixion cut off Israel's Messiah as Daniel prophesied (Daniel 9:26). Meanwhile, America has elected a "rough" leader who gets peeved at the slightest irritation referred to as "choler" in the King James Version of Scripture who is set to attack Iran.

Precisely, where are we on Nebuchadnezzar's metal statue? More accurately, our age is in the iron ankles of Nebuchadnezzar's statue's legs as it transitions into feet and toes made of iron and clay. Network news shows massive migrations of third world citizens overrunning European nations to mix with them. This is a precursor of the fulfillment of these feet of iron, representing European powers, mixing with clay which represents third world nations. America is experiencing it with Central Americans fleeing their countries to enter the USA. This has been particularly true with many in Mexico crossing into the United States illegally.

In 2016, hoards of middle easterners perished in the Mediterranean Sea as they poured onto Greece's shoreline as she was teetering on economic collapse. Being from undeveloped nations, these people represent the clay on that statue's feet as Europeans absorb them into their countries. France, Sweden, and England's citizens are complaining about this uncommon influx of families from third world countries who are unskilled in labor flooding across their boarders to merge with Europeans. They do not know that this is a portion of Bible prophecy wherein Daniel explained that they will not be successful in their assimilation stating, *"they shall mingle themselves: but they shall not cleave one to another, even as iron is not mixed with clay."* Thus, Daniel indicates there will be ethnic strife as we are seeing it erupt within these European nations that absorbed them.

Donald J. Trump the Rough Goat\He Goat King of the West

Unlike other presidents in American history, President Donald Trump did not experience a honeymoon of a time the first week he entered the White House. The day after his inauguration women protested in Washington, and when he signed legislation restricting seven Muslim countries' citizens from entering to the United States without proper vetting, the media showed protest worldwide. Within two weeks of President Trump occupying the most powerful seat in the world, presidents of Mexico and Australia called off meetings being offended by him. Other rulers proceeded with caution.

Scripture states that "the rich answer roughly." This proved true when this billionaire republican nominee faced Senator Clinton in a presidential debate, he curtly responded to Senator Clinton's comment of what she would do as president interrupted and said, "If I were president, you'd be in jail." "Scripture states that the rich answer roughly", and America's first billionaire president answers roughly and communicates directly to the American people (Prov. 18:23).

President Trump's theme song at his inaugural ball was Frank Sinatra's, *"I Did It My Way."* This man was an unstoppable force as he defied and defeated his naysayers and opponent with his goat stubborn determination. And now in fulfillment of Daniel's prophecy, President Donald Trump sits in the seat of power as King of the West; in the leadership position that will attack Persia (Iran) during his administration.

President Trump Put Persia\Iran on Notice February 8, 2017

Daniel in his prophecy wrote of a king from the west at the time of the end will be so powerful that no nation will be able to withstand him. Daniel refers to this leader's personality as *rough* and refers to him as a "goat", "rough goat," and also a "he goat" in Daniel 8:5, 8, 21. The prophet describes the western leader's temperament as being easily provoked to anger at slights and unwelcomed gestures. Prior to Donald Trump becoming president, Iran signed a nuclear pact with the Obama Administration that did not sit well with him while he ran for president. Mr. Trump cited it as one of the "worst "deals America ever signed in allowing Iran to develop nuclear capability and promised he would undo it when he became president.

On Tuesday February 7, 2017, Iran fired a short-range surface to air ballistic missile as they had under the Obama Administration. The next day, Wednesday February 8th, President Trump served Iran (Persia) notice by the United States National Security Advisor with the rough words of "As of today, we are officially putting Iran on notice." Trump fired the same security advisor the following week.

Over 2500 years ago in Iraq, Daniel foretold the next step in this parade writing that in the time of the end a king from the west would be moved with "choler" against the kings of Media and Persia and kills those leaders. The West's leader took out Saddam Hussein in 2003, and now waits for the fulfillment of its "rough" leader to take out the king of Persia known as Iran since the 1930s. When President Trump fulfills his promise of dealing with Iran, the next portion of the prophecy states that he will become "very great," and his promise to make America great again will be fulfilled.

Unfortunately, the verse in context reads, "Therefore the he goat waxed very great: and when he was **strong**, the great horn was broken; and from it came up four notable ones toward the four winds of heaven." (Daniel 8:8) Daniel explains that the horn was a king (Daniel 8:21). When this passage was fulfilled by Alexander the Great, as the Grecian king, it meant his untimely death at thirty-three years of age.

The Bible leaves a wide berth of possibilities of what this may mean for President Trump or the United States. It leaves the reader with the impression that America falls from her superpower status like Great Britain and Rome. When the great Alexander died, his superpower rulership was divided among his four generals. Since the antichrist that Daniel calls the little horn, i.e. king, did not arise out of one of his four generals' kingdoms, then this was not the fulfillment of his prophecy that he indicates would serve again "at the time of the end when transgressors are come to the full." (Daniel 8:23) Daniel was clear that his prophecy would serve "at the time of the end." So, the question is, "Are we there yet?" Read Daniel chapter 8 in the King James Version of Scripture and recall the words of Jesus rebuking those who failed to believe what was written by prophets. Regarding His resurrection, Jesus said to Jewish men, "O fools, and slow of heart to believe all that the prophets have spoken!" "Believe on the Lord Jesus Christ and you shall be saved." (Acts 16:31) Also recall that the birth of Christ was predicted, yet who were in-the-know did not bother themselves to attempt to attend His advent.

Once Power Shifts to the Mid East How Long to the End?

In the 1970s Hal Lindsey movie, *The Late Great Planet Earth,* many began predicting the coming of the Lord. The same happen in the year 2,000. Jesus stated that no one knows the day or hour of His return except God the Father (Matt. 24:36). When the West falls, Scripture gives us this ambiguous time frame in Daniel 8:22-23 of *"Now that [kingdom] being broken, whereas four stood up for it, four kingdoms shall stand up out of the nation, but not in his power.* **And in the latter time of their kingdom**, *when the transgressors are come to the full, a king of fierce countenance, who understands dark sayings, shall stand up [the antichrist]."*

Greed is not Good, it is Called a "Deadly Sin" for a Reason

Why will the West fall? "The Bible tells me so," but a more persuasive answer would be to understand that in 2008 the United States was about to plunge into a great depression. With great maneuvering, America was left unscathed, however a number of nations went bankrupt and the U.S. did not change laws which allowed for the financial industry's *greed*.

Communist Karl Marx forecasted that capitalism will fail because its nature is to feed on one of the seven deadly sins. Greed. In the 1980s, the motto seen in the movie Wall St. starring Michael Douglas that "Greed is good." God is not mocked. The United States had eight years to repent of her financial institutions' greed in allowing them to prey upon the poor. The wise King Solomon wrote a proverb that he who mocks, i.e. oppresses the poor, mocks his Maker. (Prov 17:5)

Subprime loans were used to oppress the poor while others were becoming rich and such financial antics put our nation at risk. Scripture, of which Jesus Christ said "cannot be broken" rendered this verdict. *"He that oppresses the poor to increase his riches, and he that gives to the rich, shall surely come to want (poverty)."* (Prov 22:16) When our financial institutions oppressed the poor while our government gave tax breaks to the rich, the verdict of this Scripture began to make them impoverished and it was fast becoming a reality that began to march our nation into a severe depression. But God in his mercy allowed the West a reprieve though it created a hardship worldwide due to their unprecedented greed. Yet, time was wasted during those eight years with little accomplished to remedy the lack of laws to restrict such unconscionable greed of financial oppression of the poor who only were preyed on for those subprime loans.

Billionaires & Millionaires Working 200K Government Jobs
President Donald Trump has staffed his government agencies with the wealthy. Although President Trump has the expectation of them assisting him to "Make America Great Again", the question must be asked, "Why would millionaires and billionaires take a "government job" that pays less than $300,000 a year? Did they share a moment of enlightenment and decide to give back to the American public or is their personal profit motive still at work? Since President Trump installed some of the same financial advisers that were complicit in causing the 2008 "Great Recession" that took

place suddenly while America was "strong". It may be that the same scenario of greed may be played out again by those who do not share President Trump's outlook to "Make America Great Again" but rather to increase their enormous wealth by taking shortcuts in greed. This is what communist Karl Marx wrote would be the death of American capitalism; *the greed of capitalist pigs.*

America must repent of its deadly sin of greed that gave our nation a heart attack while gas companies boasted of record profits and real estate was booming with record subprime loan sells, all the while greed was undermining the financial life of our nation when we "were strong" as it will again "when he is strong, it shall be broken." (Daniel 8:8, 22; 11:1-4 the latter verse forecast Alexander the Great but will be repeated by a stubborn goat-like king from the West in the end times.)

Scripture states that after four kingdoms split the mantle of the West's superpower and that in the latter "time of their kingdom" the antichrist will rise. Since, the Second Coming comes after his nearly seven-year reign, it will not be in our near future, though the rapture may be. The four kingdoms will assume superpower roles, then in the *latter part* of their kingdoms when transgressors are come to the full the antichrist will rise. Then there will be seven years of tribulation of such as the world has never experienced. Those seven years are represented on Nebuchadnezzar's metal statue as its feet of iron and clay. A rock from heaven smashes the statue on its feet and thus destroys this representation of mankind's government. This rock from heaven represents the Second Coming of Jesus Christ who will reign for 1,000 years.

John, author of Revelation, had this to say of Jesus after He had risen from the dead and ascended to sit at the right hand of God as Daniel 7:13 and Psalms 110 foretold. John wrote that "He was in the world, and the world was made by him, and the world knew him not." (John 1:10)

Jesus was the promised "seed of the woman" that God told Eve He would use to crush the head of the serpent, being Satan. Since women do not have "seed" i.e. sperm, this was indicative that the seed of the woman would be born of God as it happened through the Virgin Mary's womb. He was called *Emmanuel* being interpreted "God with us" and He declared that He and His Father were one. (John 10:30)

"For God so loved the world that he gave his only begotten son that whosoever believes on him shall not perish but have everlasting life." (John 3:16) "Believest thou this?" **If not, then prepare for the following to happen in your lifetime. You can see it taking shape today.**

Section Three: The Tribulation Period Begins

Prophecy No. 11
The Tribulation Period Begins
"For then shall be great tribulation, such as was not since the beginning of the world to this time, no, nor ever shall be. And except those days be shortened [by His 2nd Coming], there should no flesh be saved: but for the elect's [Israel's] sake those days shall be shortened." (Jesus – Matthew 24:21-22)

✓ The Tribulation Period is called "the time of Jacob's [Israel's] trouble." (Jeremiah 30:7)

✓ The Tribulation Period will last approximately seven years.

✓ This period in time is also known as The Great Tribulation.

Prophecy No. 12
Four Horsemen of the Apocalypse will be Released

The First Horseman: The Anti-Semite
Antichrist\Antimessiah
"When the Lamb opened one of the seals, I heard, as it were a noise of thunder... And I saw and behold a white horse: and he that sat on him had a bow: and a crown was given to him: and he went forth conquering, and to conquer." (Revelation 6:2)

This horseman is the Anti-Semite *Antichrist\Antimessiah*; the coming global ruler of the world from the Middle East who shall come to power by peaceful means. (See Section Six entitled "The Anti-Semite Antichrist\Antimessiah")

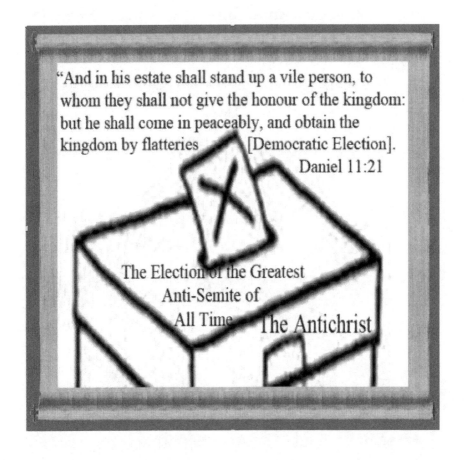

"And in his estate shall stand up a vile person, to whom they shall not give the honour of the kingdom: but he shall come in peaceably, and obtain the kingdom by flatteries [Democratic Election].
Daniel 11:21

The Election of the Greatest Anti-Semite of All Time The Antichrist

Prophecy No. 13

World Leaders Announce Terrorism Dismantled Prior to Nuclear Holocaust

"For yourselves know perfectly that the day of the Lord so cometh as a thief in the night. **For when they shall say, Peace and safety; then sudden destruction cometh upon them**, as travail upon a woman with child; and they shall not escape. ☐But ye, brethren, are not in darkness, that that day should overtake you as a thief." (1 Thessalonians 5:2-4)

✓ The announcement of "peace and safety" will be brought about when the major leaders of terrorist organizations are apprehended and all terror cells such as Al-Qaeda, ISIS, the Taliban, Hezbollah, Hamas, the PLO, Al-Shabaab, and Boko Haram are disbanded. These word "Peace and safety," which are world craves to hear will be the detonation fuse of the "sudden destruction" that will impact the world. "Believe on the Lord Jesus Christ and thou shall be saved..." (Acts 16:31)

Prophecy No. 14

War is Unleashed Upon the Earth

The Second Horseman: War

"And when he had opened the second seal there went out another horse that was red: and power was given to him that sat thereon to take peace from the earth, and that they should kill one another: and there was given to him a great sword." This red horse represents *war*. (Revelation 6: 3-4)

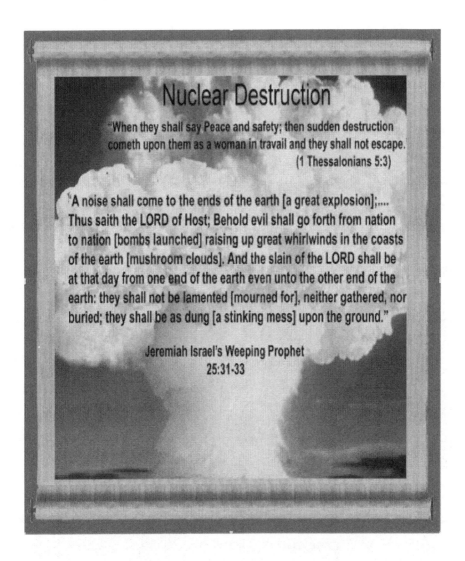

Nuclear Destruction

"When they shall say Peace and safety; then sudden destruction cometh upon them as a woman in travail and they shall not escape.
(1 Thessalonians 5:3)

"A noise shall come to the ends of the earth [a great explosion];.... Thus saith the LORD of Host; Behold evil shall go forth from nation to nation [bombs launched] raising up great whirlwinds in the coasts of the earth [mushroom clouds]. And the slain of the LORD shall be at that day from one end of the earth even unto the other end of the earth: they shall not be lamented [mourned for], neither gathered, nor buried; they shall be as dung [a stinking mess] upon the ground."

Jeremiah Israel's Weeping Prophet
25:31-33

Prophecy No. 15
Weapons of Mass Destruction Unleashed
And except those days should be shortened [by His 2nd Coming], there should no flesh be saved [alive upon the earth], but for the elect's sake [the Israelis' sake] those days shall be shortened:" (Matthew 24:22)

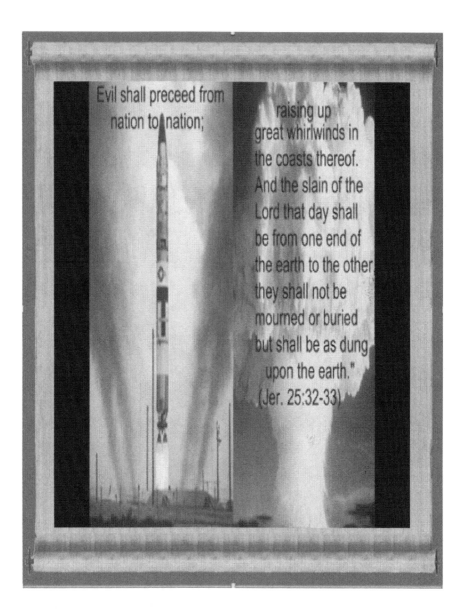

> Evil shall preceed from nation to nation; raising up great whirlwinds in the coasts thereof. And the slain of the Lord that day shall be from one end of the earth to the other they shall not be mourned or buried but shall be as dung upon the earth." (Jer. 25:32-33)

"The anger of the LORD will not turn back until he hath performed the thoughts of his heart: **in the latter days you shall consider it perfectly**...." (Jeremiah 23:20)

"And I will grant wonders in the sky above And signs on the earth below, Blood, and fire, and **vapor of smoke**." (Acts 2:19)

"A noise shall come even to the ends of the earth [an explosion]; for the LORD hath a controversy with the nations, he will plead with them. Behold, evil shall go forth from nation to nation [missiles launched], and a great whirlwind shall be raised up from the coasts of the earth [nuclear clouds]. And the slain of the LORD shall be at that day from one end of the earth even unto the other end of the earth [millions of people dead]: they shall not be lamented, neither gathered, nor buried; they shall be dung upon the ground." (Jeremiah 25:31-33 KJV)

Prophecy No. 16
National Leaders Perplexed
"And there shall be signs … upon the earth distress of nations, with perplexity…" (Luke 21:25)

✓ International leaders did not know what to due in the 2008 economic international stock market crash. More to come.

Prophecy No. 17
Nuclear Bombs Disintegrates Bodies
"And this shall be the plague wherewith the LORD will smite all the people that have fought against Jerusalem; Their flesh shall *consume away* while they stand upon their feet [before they hit the ground], and their eyes shall *consume away* in their holes, and their tongue shall *consume away* in their mouth." (Zechariah 14:12)

✓ "They have seduced my people, saying, Peace; and there was no peace." (Ezekiel 13:10)

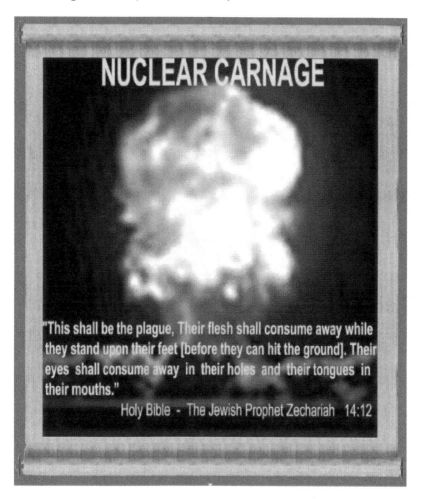

Prophecy No. 18
Dust From Nuclear Blast to Block Sunlight
"And it shall come to pass in that day, saith the Lord GOD, that I will cause the sun to go down at noon, and I will darken the earth in the clear day:" (The Prophet Amos 8:9)

Prophecy No. 19
Radiation to Cause Baldness on All Heads on Earth

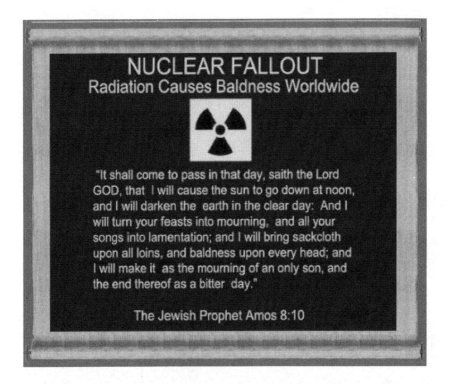

"And I will turn your feasts into mourning, and all your songs into lamentation; and I will bring up sackcloth upon all loins, and baldness upon every head; and I will make it as the mourning of an only son, and the end thereof as a bitter day." (Amos 8:10)

Prophecy No. 20
Plague of Hail Nuclear Winter Caused by Nuclear War

NUCLEAR WINTER
Produces Great Hailstones

"And there fell upon men a great hail out of heaven, every stone about the weight of a talent [58 lbs] and men blasphemed God because of the plague of the hail; for the plague thereof was exceeding great." (Revelation 16:21)

"And there fell upon men a great hail out of heaven, every stone about the weight of a talent [58 lbs.]: and men blasphemed God because of the plague of the hail; for the plague thereof was exceeding great." (Revelation 16:21)

Prophecy No. 21
Radiation Makes Certain Lands Uninhabitable

"For it is the day of the LORD's vengeance, and the year of recompenses for the controversy of Zion. And the streams thereof shall be turned into pitch, and the dust thereof into brimstone, and the land thereof shall become burning pitch. It shall not be quenched night nor day; **the smoke thereof shall go up for ever:** from generation to generation **it shall lie waste; none shall pass through it for ever and ever."** (Isaiah 34:8-10)

"And it shall come to pass, when seventy years are accomplished, that I will punish the king of Babylon, and that nation, saith the LORD, for their iniquity, and the land of the Chaldeans, and will make it **perpetual desolations**." (Jer. 25:12)

"For I have sworn by myself, saith the LORD, that Bozrah shall become a desolation, a reproach, a waste, and a curse; and all the cities thereof shall be **perpetual wastes**." (Jer. 49:13)

"And **the land of Egypt shall be desolate and waste**; and they shall know that I am the LORD:... Behold, therefore I am against thee, and against thy rivers, and **I will make the land of Egypt utterly waste and desolate**, from the tower of Syene even unto the border of Ethiopia." (Ezek. 29:9-10)

✓ The earth will last 1,000 years after Christ's return. The half-life of radiation will prevent anyone from passing through its contaminated lands "for ever and ever."

Prophecy No. 22
The Most Terrible Famine in World History
The Third Horseman: World Famine

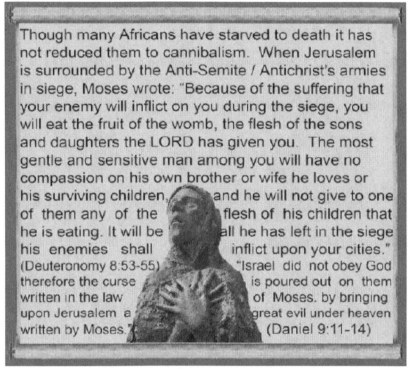

Though many Africans have starved to death it has not reduced them to cannibalism. When Jerusalem is surrounded by the Anti-Semite / Antichrist's armies in siege, Moses wrote: "Because of the suffering that your enemy will inflict on you during the siege, you will eat the fruit of the womb, the flesh of the sons and daughters the LORD has given you. The most gentle and sensitive man among you will have no compassion on his own brother or wife he loves or his surviving children, and he will not give to one of them any of the flesh of his children that he is eating. It will be all he has left in the siege his enemies shall inflict upon your cities." (Deuteronomy 8:53-55) "Israel did not obey God therefore the curse is poured out on them written in the law of Moses. by bringing upon Jerusalem a great evil under heaven written by Moses." (Daniel 9:11-14)

"...when he had opened the third seal... I beheld a black horse; and he that sat on him had a pair of balances in his hand. And I heard a voice in the midst of the four beasts say, A measure of wheat for a penny, and three measures of barley for a penny; and see that ye not hurt the oil or the wine." This horseman represents *famine* (food shortages).(Revelation 6:5-6)

✓ Climate change will cause drought resulting in crop failure and famine. As farms grow corn for vehicle consumption, this will compete with human hunger.

✓ Pollenating honey bees in the United States are dying

Prophecy No. 23
Men Eating Their Own Flesh and Blood To Survive

"And he shall snatch on the right hand, and be hungry; and he shall eat on the left hand, and they shall not be satisfied: they shall eat every man the flesh of his own arm:" (Isaiah 9:20)

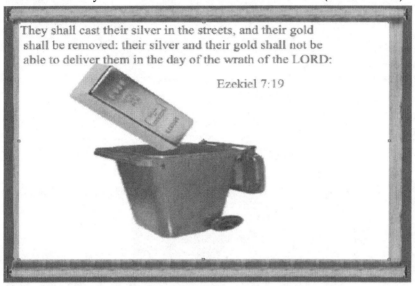

They shall cast their silver in the streets, and their gold shall be removed: their silver and their gold shall not be able to deliver them in the day of the wrath of the LORD:

Ezekiel 7:19

During hurricane Katrina in New Orleans, people with pockets full of money could not buy a bottle of water. Money will hold no value in these times.

Prophecy No. 24
No Escape from Either Pestilences, War, or Famine and Money will be Worthless

"Ye shall hear of wars rumors of war: see that ye be not troubled: for all these things must come to pass, but the end is not yet." (Matthew 23:6)

"The sword is without [outside Jerusalem], and the pestilence and the famine within [inside Jerusalem]: he that is in the field shall die with the sword; and he that is in the city, famine and pestilence shall devour him. But they that escape of them shall escape, and shall be on the mountains like doves of the valleys, all of them mourning, every one for his iniquity.☐☐☐All hands shall be feeble, and all knees shall be weak as water.☐☐Horror shall cover them; and shame shall be upon all faces, and baldness upon all their heads [due to radiation]. They shall cast their silver in the streets, and their gold shall be removed: their silver and their gold shall not be able to deliver them in the day of the wrath of the LORD: they shall not satisfy their souls, neither fill their bowels..." (Ezekiel 7:15-19)

✓ Hunger riots will occur

Section Four: Global Scale Mass Destruction

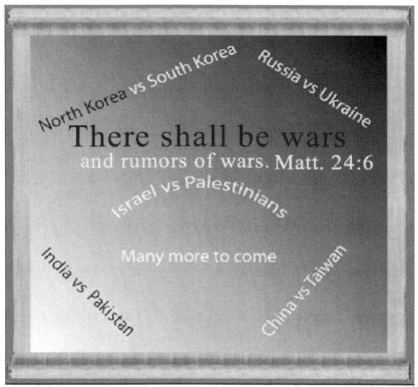

Prophecy No. 25
One Fourth of the World's Population is Killed

The Fourth Horseman: Death

"And when he had opened the fourth seal...I looked and behold a pale horse: and his name that sat on him was Death, and Hell followed with him. And power was given unto them over a fourth part [25 percent] of the earth, to kill them with sword, and with hunger, and with death..." (Revelation 6:7-8)

8 billion people times 25% = 2 billion people dead

Prophecy No. 26
Asteroid hits Earth & Dust to Block Sun
"And the fifth angel sounded, and I saw a star fall from heaven unto the earth: [an asteroid] and… the sun and the air were darkened…" (Revelation 9:1-2)

✓ Scientists believe this may be how the Dinosaur Age ended.

Prophecy No. 27
Asteroids Spray Earth then a Great Earthquake
"…When he had opened the sixth seal…And the stars of heaven fell unto the earth, [asteroids] even as a fig tree casteth her untimely figs, when she is shaken of a mighty wind…. There was a great earthquake; and the sun became black as sackcloth of hair, and the moon became as blood; …And the kings of the earth, and the great men, and the rich men, and the chief captains, and the mighty men, and every bondman [slave], and every free man, hid themselves in the dens and in the rocks of the mountains. And said to the mountains and rocks, Fall on us, and hide us from the face of him that sitteth on the throne, and from the wrath of the Lamb. For the great day of his wrath hath come; and who shall be able to stand?" (Revelation 6:12-17)

✓   Notice that slavery is prophesied to be active during the end times. CNN and the BBC are airing stories increasing in frequency of reports that slavery has revived in foreign lands such as in Africa, China, and India.

✓ Per CNN and the *New York Times,* the earth is on near collision courses with asteroids in the years 2014, 2028, and 2029. For this cause, the United States space program has launched missions for the purpose of gathering information on such threatening asteroids. Our solar system may pass through a dangerous portion of our galaxy that may yield the "signs in the sun, and in the moon, and in the stars" that Christ spoke of, so get your telescopes ready. (Luke 21:25) Recall Jupiter was struck by a comet in 1994.

✓ Ironically, everyone on earth during this time will believe that Jesus the Christ, *the Passover Lamb of God,* is the one bringing these plagues upon all the inhabitants of the earth who refuse to accept His offering to be their Savior. They shall flee from Him, the wrath of the Lamb. (Revelation 6:16)

Prophecy No. 28
The Seventh Seal Opened

"When he [Jesus] had opened the seventh seal there was silence in heaven for a half an hour… then there was thunderings, lightnings, and an earthquake. And the seven angels with seven trumpets prepared themselves to sound." (Revelation 8:1-6)

Prophecy No. 29
Trumpets Judgment Atmosphere Attacks Plant Life
"The first angel sounded, and there followed hail and fire mingled with blood, and they were cast upon the earth: and the third part of trees was burnt up, and all green grass was burnt up." (Revelation 8:7)

Prophecy No. 30
Asteroid Falls into the Sea 1/3 of Sea Life Perishes
"And the second angel sounded, and as it were a great mountain burning with fire was cast into the sea [an asteroid]: and the third part of the sea became blood;☐And the third part of the creatures which were in the sea, and had life, died; and the third part of the ships were destroyed." (Revelation 8:8-9)

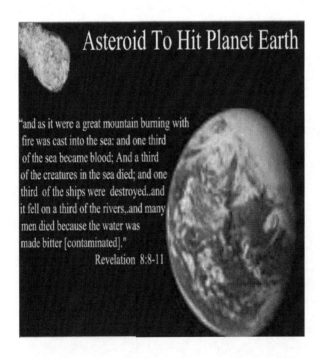

Asteroid To Hit Planet Earth

"and as it were a great mountain burning with fire was cast into the sea: and one third of the sea became blood; And a third of the creatures in the sea died; and one third of the ships were destroyed..and it fell on a third of the rivers,..and many men died because the water was made bitter [contaminated]."
Revelation 8:8-11

✓　Many NASA space scientists, who will be able to see these prophesied events, work under a gag order on what information they can disclose to the general public.

✓　President Obama ended the space program to divert funds to develop an asteroid destroying weapon, but in February 2011 242 House Republicans voted Wednesday to repeal the Asteroid Destruction and American Preservation Act, stating that it was a massive waste of tax payers money. See links:

https://www.scientificamerican.com/article/trump-rsquo-s-nasa-budget-eliminates-crewed-mission-to-asteroid/

http://www.cbsnews.com/news/japan-launches-asteroid-blasting-space-probe/

http://www.newyorker.com/tech/elements/age-asteroids

Prophecy No. 31
One Third of Earth's Fresh Water is Contaminated
"And the third angel sounded, and there fell a great star from heaven, burning as it were a lamp, and it fell upon the third part of the rivers, and upon the fountains of waters; And the name of the star is called Wormwood: and the third part of the waters became wormwood; and many men died of the waters, because they were made bitter [contaminated]." (Revelation 8:10-11)

✓　**Wormwood means bitter (Chernobyl in Russian)**

Prophecy No. 32
Heart Attacks Brought on by Fear

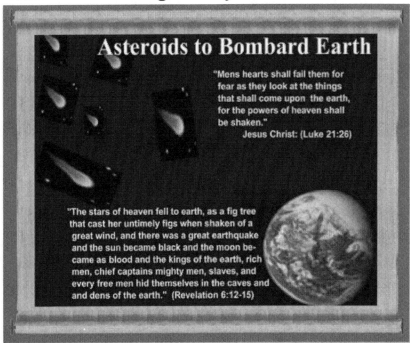

Asteroids to Bombard Earth

"Mens hearts shall fail them for fear as they look at the things that shall come upon the earth, for the powers of heaven shall be shaken."
Jesus Christ: (Luke 21:26)

"The stars of heaven fell to earth, as a fig tree that cast her untimely figs when shaken of a great wind, and there was a great earthquake and the sun became black and the moon became as blood and the kings of the earth, rich men, chief captains mighty men, slaves, and every free men hid themselves in the caves and and dens of the earth." (Revelation 6:12-15)

"Men's hearts failing them for fear, and for looking after those things which are coming on the earth: for the powers of heaven shall be shaken." (Jesus Christ – Luke 21:26)

✓ What's more fearful than watching an approaching asteroid(s) on a collision course with planet Earth after surviving previous Asteroid strikes?

Once a bomb is exploded in space, to save the world from an asteroid, this explosion will shake "the powers of heaven" and will have an horrific effect on the stability of space and the Bible predicts that stars will fall into earth's atmosphere and to the ground as a untimely wind blows against a fig tree and its figs fall to the ground. As the populations of the advanced world are lengthening their longevity, there will be hosts of heart attacks and strokes that will cause many people to die of fear "for looking at those things which are coming on the earth."

Prophecy No. 33
The Skies Are Darkened

"And the fourth angel sounded, and the third part of the sun was smitten, and the third part of the moon, and the third part of the stars; so as the third part of them was darkened, and the day shone not for a third part of it [eight hours], and the night likewise. And I beheld, and heard an angel flying through the midst of heaven, saying with a loud voice, Woe, woe, woe, to the inhibiters of the earth by reason of the other voices of the trumpet of the three angels, which are yet to sound!" (Revelation 8:12-13)

Prophecy No. 34
Oxygen Supply Divinely Protected

"And the fifth angel sounded, and I saw a star fall from heaven unto the earth: [another asteroid] and ... the sun and the air were darkened by reason of the smoke ... And there came out of the smoke locusts upon the earth: and unto them was given power, as the scorpions of the earth have power. And it was commanded them that they should not hurt the grass of the earth, neither any green thing [the oxygen supplies], neither any tree; but only those men which have not the seal of God in their foreheads. And to them it was given that they should not kill them, but that they should be tormented five months: and their torment was as the torment of a scorpion, when he striketh a man. And in those days shall men seek death, and shall not find it; and shall desire to die, and death shall flee from them." (Revelation 9:1-6)

Prophecy No. 35
New Locust Life Forms Emerge

"And the shapes of the locusts were like unto horses prepared unto battle; and on their heads were as it were crowns like gold, and their faces were as the faces of men. And they had hair as the hair of women, and their teeth were as the teeth of lions. And they had breastplates, as it were breastplates of iron; and the sound of their wings was as the sound of chariots of many horses running to battle. And they had tails like unto scorpions, and there were stings in their tails: and their power was to hurt men five months." (Revelation 9:7-10)

✓   It is speculative but noteworthy that some believe that this may be a crude ancient description of manned green army helicopters firing bullets.

Prophecy No. 36
200 Million Army Cross Iraq's Euphrates Riverbed

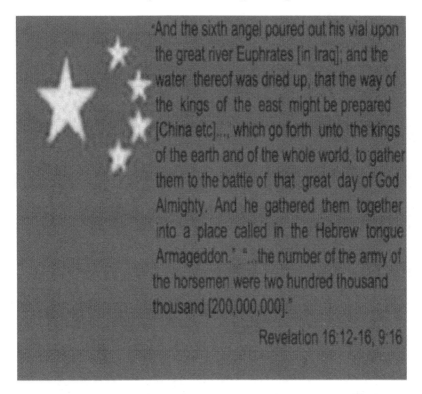

"And the sixth angel poured out his vial upon the great river Euphrates [in Iraq]; and the water thereof was dried up, that the way of the kings of the east might be prepared [China etc]..., which go forth unto the kings of the earth and of the whole world, to gather them to the battle of that great day of God Almighty. And he gathered them together into a place called in the Hebrew tongue Armageddon." "...the number of the army of the horsemen were two hundred thousand thousand [200,000,000]."

Revelation 16:12-16, 9:16

"And the sixth angel poured out his vial upon the great river Euphrates; and the water thereof was dried up, that the way of the kings of the east might be prepared.... One woe is past; and, behold, there come two woes more hereafter. And the sixth angel sounded, and I heard a voice ...which is before God, saying to the sixth angel which had the trumpet, Loose the four angels which are bound in the great river Euphrates.

And the four angels were loosed, which were prepared for an hour, and a day, and a month, and a year, for to slay the third part of men [2.3 billion presently]. And the number of the army of the horsemen were two hundred thousand thousand [200 million man army]: and I heard the number of them. By these three was the third part of men killed [1/3 of worlds population] by the fire, and by the smoke, and by the brimstone..." (Revelation 16:12, 9:12-16, 18)

Prophecy No. 37
Widespread Drug Abuse

"And the rest of the men which were not killed by these plagues yet repented not of the works of their hands, that they should not worship devils, and idols of gold, and silver, and brass, and stone, and of wood: which neither can see, nor hear, nor walk: Neither repented they of their murders, nor of their sorceries [translated from the Greek word: *pharmacia* i.e., drug abuse] nor of their fornication, nor of their thefts [looting]." (Revelation 20:21)

When Hurricane Katrina hit New Orleans, the world was given another miniature picture of how people will behave in the midst of catastrophic events.

"And the rest of the men which were not killed by these plagues yet repented not of the works of their hands, that they should not worship devils, and idols of gold, and silver, and brass, and stone, and of wood: which neither can see, nor hear, nor walk: Neither repented they of their murders, nor of their sorceries [pharmacia i.e., drugs] nor of their fornication, nor of their thefts [looting]."

(Revelation 20:21)

✓   The Greek word translated sorceries was *pharmacia* from whence we get the word *pharmacy* in regards to drugs. Hence, they will not repent of their drug abuse.

✓   Notice all these plagues are centered in the East; in the orient where men still worship idols of gold, stone, and silver. The horn of the western power structure is destroyed according to Daniel Chapter 8 which will result in murders, drug abuse, and looting. This is none other than a primitive description of anarchy, the total breakdown of government.

Section Five: The Seven Last Plagues

Prophecy No. 38 Global Warming Peaks

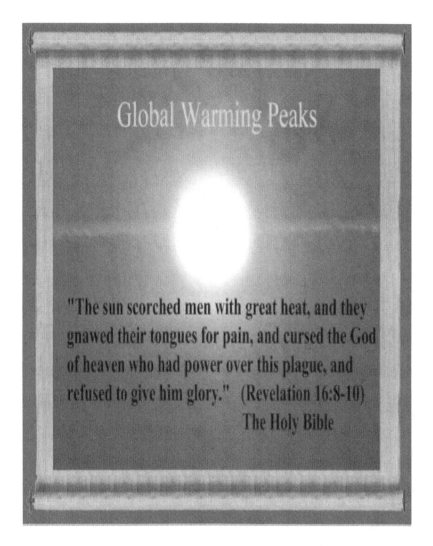

"And the fourth angel poured out his vial upon the sun; and power was given unto him to scorch men with fire. And men were scorched with great heat, and blasphemed the name of

God, which hath power over these plagues: and they repented not to give him glory." (Revelation 16:8-9)

Prophecy No. 39
Seven Vials of The Wrath of God Poured on Earth

"And I heard a great voice out of the temple [in heaven] saying to the seven angels, Go your ways, and pour out the vials of the wrath of God upon the earth. □And the first went, and poured out his vial upon the earth; and there fell a noisome and grievous sore upon the men which had the mark of the beast [666 or his name], and upon them which worshipped his image." (Revelation 16:1-2) [See Section six: The Anti-Semite Antichrist\Antimessiah called the Beast in Scripture]

Prophecy No. 40
Much Sea Life Destroyed

"And the second angel poured out his vial upon the sea; and it became as the blood of a dead man: and every living soul died in the sea." (Revelation 16:3)

✓ Notice that mankind will not acknowledge God as responsible for global warming peaking. Man will continue to give glory to pollution, greenhouse gases, cow flatulence, and etc. rather than to Almighty God who has power over this

plague. Men will with their gnawed tongues curse God's name rather than repent (turn away from) their ungodly deeds and place faith in Jesus His Son for salvation.

Prophecy No. 41
Painful Sores & Darkness Throughout the Earth
"And the fifth angel poured out his vial upon the seat of the beast [the throne of the Anti-Semite Antichrist\Antimessiah]; and his kingdom was full of darkness; and they gnawed their tongues for pain.   And blasphemed the God of heaven because of their pains and their sores, and repented not of their deeds." (Revelation 16:10-11)

✓   Man is God's only creation that resists Him. Lion's cry to God for prey. (Ps. 104:21)   Baby birds cry to God for their food. (Job 38:41) The sun and moon and "the sweet influences of Pleiades [a constellation]" obey God by staying in their assigned orbits. (Jer. 31:35-36, Job 38:31)   The sea obeys His command for its waves come to the shore but not wash over the earth. (Jer. 5:22) Only man refuses to acknowledge or obey his Creator. As it is written, "The fool says in his heart, "*There is* no God."" (Psalms 14:1) In the King James Version of the Bible italicized words were added by the translators to let the reader know that they were not in the original text but were added to assist the reader. Therefore, a more authentic rendering of this verse without its italicized word is: "The fool says in his heart, "No God." Stark disobedience.

Prophecy No. 42
Armies of the East Summoned to Armageddon
"And the sixth angel poured out his vial upon the great river Euphrates [in Iraq]; and the water thereof was dried up, that the way of the kings of the east might be prepared i.e. China and etc. For they are the spirits of devils, working miracles, which go forth unto the kings of the earth and of the whole

world, to gather them to the battle of that great day of God Almighty. And he gathered them together into a place called in the Hebrew tongue Armageddon." (Revelation 16:12-16)

✓ **Armageddon is an actual place. It is a vast serene valley located in Israel.**

Prophecy No. 44
The Greatest Earthquake in the World

"And the seventh angel poured out his vial into the air;... And there were voices, and thunders, and lightnings; and there was a great earthquake, such as was not since men were upon the earth, so mighty an earthquake, and so great.... And the cities of the nations fell." (Revelation 16:17-19)

✓ "The earth shall reel to and fro like a drunkard." (Isaiah 24:20)

✓ "And they shall go into the holes of the rocks, and into the caves of the earth, for fear of the LORD... when he [God] ariseth to shake terribly the earth." (Isaiah 2:19)

Prophecy No. 45

Seven Horrors Yet to be Revealed

"And I saw another mighty angel come down from heaven... and he set his right foot upon the sea, and his left foot on the earth, And cried with a loud voice, as when a lion roareth: and when he had cried, seven thunders uttered their voices. ☐And when the seven thunders had uttered their voices, I was about to write: and I heard a voice from heaven saying unto me, Seal up those things which the seven thunders uttered, and write them not." (Revelation 10:1-4)

Seven dreadful plagues John was forbidden to write down.

1. _____

2. _____

3. _____

4. _____

5. _____

6. _____

7. _____

The Next Section Is About the "Superman" That The World Awaits Today. He Will Settle The Present Mid-East Crisis. The Bible Refers To Him by names such As The Beast, The Man of Sin, That Wicked, The Son of Perdition (Hell), The Assyrian, The Little Horn, And The Antichrist Who Will Prove to be the Greatest Anti-Semite who Ever Lived and His Number is Six-Six-Six (666).

Section Six: An Anti-Semite Anti-Messiah will be the Antichrist

The Destabilization of Persia (Iran) by the West

Until 1939, Persia was the name of what is now called Iraq. According to the eighth chapter of Daniel's prophecy, in the last days a king from the West, called a he goat, will be moved to attack the present day Persian Gulf provinces known as Iraq and Iran called Assyria, Babylon, Media, and Persia in ancient times. This western king will attack with "choler," meaning hostile anger, destabilizing the Persian Gulf region by stomping its kings to residue. (Daniel 8:3-5) Afterwards, several leaders will rise and fall in the Persian Gulf region. Then a leader referred to in Scripture as "the little horn" will not be given the kingdom at first, but will eventually obtain it "by flatteries [a democratic process], and by peace shall he destroy many." (Daniel 8:25, 11:21, 32) Americans can rest assured that democracy will be established in the Gulf region. Prophets Jeremiah and Daniel wrote that a flattery elected politician of "fierce countenance" in the Mid-East will be a destroyer of *the gentiles.*" (Jer. 4:7, Dan. 8:23) In the King James Version of the Bible the word "gentiles" was the term Moses, Christ, and Paul used in referencing Europeans, whose father was Noah's firstborn son, Japheth the Elder, father of the Caucasians. (Genesis 10:5, 21) Christ also referred to the Europeans of the Roman Empire as "the gentiles." (Mark 10:33-34) Paul was an apostle to the gentiles, i.e. Europeans.

Christ called the times in which we live "the time of the gentiles" in which Europeans will rule the world. Unfortunately, at the end of European world-domination called "the times of the gentiles" in Scripture, a Middle Easterner referred to as "the Beast" is prophesied to be "a destroyer of the gentiles." (Jeremiah 4:7) America and Great Britain have stirred the proverbial pot of anti-European sentiments in the Arab world and gulf region. Therefore, Jeremiah's prophecy of "The destroyer of the gentiles is on his way" is no longer farfetched.

Prophecy No. 46
The Anti-Semite/Antichrist Will Not Know That He Is the Rod of God's Anger

"O Assyrian [O Persian], the rod of mine anger, and the staff in their hand is mine indignation. I will send him against an hypocritical nation, and against the people of my wrath [the time of Jacob's (Israel's) trouble] will I give him a charge, to take the spoil, and to take the prey, and to tread them down like the mire of the streets. Howbeit <u>he meaneth not so, neither doth his heart think so; but it is in his heart to destroy and cut off nations not a few</u>." (Isaiah 10:5-7)

✓ "The destroyer of the gentiles is on his way. He is gone forth from his place to make thy land desolate; and thy cities shall be laid waste, without inhabitant. For this gird you [yourself] with sackcloth, lament and howl: for the fierce anger of the LORD is not turned back from us." (Jeremiah 4:7-8)

Prophecy No. 47
Three Rulers of the Destabilized Middle East Region Will Come to Power Prior to the Rise of the Greatest Anti-Semite Ever, known as the Antichrist

"And now will I shew thee the truth. Behold, there shall stand up yet three kings in Persia [present day Iraq and Iran]; and the fourth shall be far richer than they all [the Anti-Semite / Antichrist]: and by his strength through his riches he shall stir up all against the realm of Grecia [Europe, and the king of the west]." (Daniel 11:2)

Prophecy No. 48
The First of Persian Gulf's Last Four Rulers (Saddam Hussein)

"And a mighty king shall stand up, that shall rule with great dominion, and do according to his will. ☐And when he shall stand up, his kingdom shall be broken, and shall be divided toward the four winds of heaven; and not to his posterity [his sons or daughters], nor according to his dominion which he ruled: for his kingdom shall be plucked up, even for others beside those." (Daniel 11:3-4)

✓ Saddam Hussein's male posterity [sons, Uday and Qusay] were killed in war with the King of the West, neither did his surviving daughters inherit his throne.

Prophecy No. 49

Second Ruler of Persian Gulf Marries a Princess in a Peace Agreement and Offspring to Wage War

"And the king of the south [Arabia] shall be strong, and one of his princes; and he shall be strong above him, and have dominion; his dominion shall be a great dominion. □⁶And in the end of years they shall join themselves together; for the king's daughter of the south shall come to the king of the north to make an agreement: but she shall not retain the power of the arm; neither shall he stand, nor his arm: but she shall be given up, and they that brought her, and he that begat her, and he that strengthened her in these times. □⁷But out of a branch of her roots shall one stand up in his estate, which shall come with an army, and shall enter into the fortress of the king of the north, and shall deal against them, and shall prevail:....and he shall continue more years than the king of the north." (Daniel 11:5-8)

Prophecy No. 50

Mid-East Rulers Shall War Over Gulf Region

"So the king of the south shall come into his kingdom, and shall return into his own land. ¹⁰But his sons shall be stirred up, and shall assemble a multitude of great forces: and one shall certainly come, and overflow, and pass through: then shall he return, and be stirred up, even to his fortress. □¹¹And the king of the south shall be moved with choler, and shall come forth and fight with him, even with the king of the north: and he shall set forth a great multitude; but the multitude shall be given into his hand. [12]And when he hath taken away the multitude, his heart shall be lifted up; and he shall cast down many ten thousands: but he shall not be strengthened by it." (Daniel 11:9-12)

Prophecy No. 51
Second Ruler of Gulf Regionto be Defeated in during Many Years of War

"For the king of the north shall return, and shall set forth a multitude greater than the former, and shall certainly come <u>after certain years</u> with a great army and with much riches. Read the rest in (Daniel 11:13-19)

✓ Notice that there will be a passage of many "years." This is why the Scriptures state that there shall be wars and rumor of wars, "but the end is not yet." (Matt. 24:6) The "Arab Spring" of the upheavals in of civil wars in Egypt, Libya, Yemen, Syria and more was what is being called the Arab Spring. We still have years ahead of us, but prophecies will continue being fulfilled albeit at a much slower pace.

Prophecy No. 52
Third Gulf Region Ruler Raises Taxes to Restore Its Infrastructure but will Die of Natural Causes
The third ruler will "stand up in his estate a raiser of taxes in the glory of the kingdom, but within few days he shall be destroyed, neither in anger, nor in battle." (Daniel 11:20)

✓ Taxes will be raised to repair the infrastructure destroyed by the west as well as to finance their army. This may indicate that the West will not finance the rebuilding of the Gulf's Region infrastructure.

Prophecy No. 53
The Belief System of the Anti-Semite /Antichrist

"Neither shall he regard the God of his fathers, nor the desire of women, nor regard any god: for he shall magnify himself above all." (Daniel 11:37)

✓ Whether he will be homosexual or just so committed to his aims is unknown, but his desire will not be toward women according to Daniel's prophecy.

✓ Although Christians refer to the coming of this greatest of Anti- Semites as the Antichrist, he will be against all religions; not regarding any god.

Prophecy No. 54
The Anti-Semite/ Antichrist Honors a Strange God

Prior to his assassination, "Shall he honor the God of forces [a higher power]: and a god whom his fathers knew not shall he honor with gold, and silver, and with precious stones, and pleasant things. Thus shall he do … with a strange god, whom he shall acknowledge and increase with glory…" (Daniel 11:38-39)

Prophecy No. 55
The Anti-Semite/Antichrist Brings Peace Covenant to the Middle East

"...he shall magnify himself in his heart, and by peace shall destroy many." (Daniel 8:25) "And after the league [covenant] made with him he shall work deceitfully [betrayal]: for he shall come up, and shall become strong with a small people."(Daniel 11:23)

✓ The small gangs are in the Mideast are vying for power.

"And through his policy also he shall cause craft to prosper in his hand..." (Daniel 8:25)

✓ His policy of peace will begin by bringing peace to the Middle East beginning with Israel and the Arab states. The agreement (covenant of peace) will be that for seven years (a week as Daniel describes it), wherein Israel will agree not to invade Arab occupied territories, and for seven years the Arab nations will agree not to invade Israel.

Prophecy No. 56
Solomon's Temple to be Rebuilt on Temple Mount
"But the court which is without the temple leave out, and measure it not; for it is given unto the Gentiles:..." (Revelation 11:2)

A Muslim house of worship called the Dome of the Rock is presently located on the Temple Mount in the area where the Court of the Gentiles was located in previous Jewish temple. Therefore, it will be permissible for this Muslim shrine to remain in this area when the Jewish temple is rebuilt.

Orthodox Jews will reinitiate the daily animal sacrifices of lambs, bulls, goats, and doves in the rebuilt Jewish temple. (Daniel 9:27)

The first 3 ½ years will be peaceful and world prosperity will reign, but in "the middle of the week" (3 ½ years) the Anti-Semite / Antichrist will break this covenant himself after his attempted assassination. (Daniel 9:27)

Prophecy No. 57
The Assassination of the Antichrist

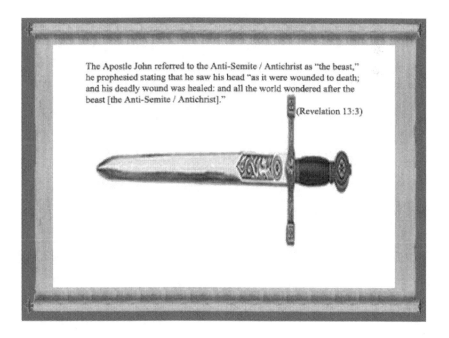

The Apostle John referred to the Anti-Semite / Antichrist as "the beast," he prophesied stating that he saw his head "as it were wounded to death; and his deadly wound was healed: and all the world wondered after the beast [the Anti-Semite / Antichrist]."

(Revelation 13:3)

The Apostle John referred to the Anti-Semite / Antichrist as "the beast," he prophesied "and I saw one of his heads as it were wounded to death; and his deadly wound was healed: and all the world wondered after the beast [the Anti-Semite / Antichrist]." (Revelation 13:3)

✓ This is the Anti-Semite/Antichrist's mock resurrection of Jesus Christ. When he is "resurrected," he will break the covenant with Israel and go into the rebuilt temple and declare himself God, who has been raised from the dead. (1 Thessalonians 2:5)

✓ In keeping with history, any Arab leader who attempts to make peace with Israel is assassinated, i.e., Egypt's Anwar Sadat who attempted peace with Israel former Prime Minister Menachem Begin, and King Abdullah of Jordan who attempted peace with former Israeli Prime Minister Golda Meir. In the peace negotiations that were moderated by, then, President Bill Clinton, PLO President Yassar Arafat balked at an agreeable peace plan with Israeli Prime Minister Yitzhak Rabin possibly for this reason.

Prophecy No. 58
A Post-Rapture Pope Encourages Worship of Antichrist After His "Resurrection"

After the Anti-Semite / Antichrist's mock resurrection, a religious figure that the Scriptures call "the false prophet" will arise and occupy the position of Pope in the Catholic (Universal) Church that is left on earth after *the rapture* (See Prophecy No. 150).

He will "causeth the earth and them which dwell therein to worship the beast [the Anti-Semite / Antichrist] whose deadly wound was healed." (Revelation 13:12)

Prophecy No. 59
Post-Rapture Pope, "The False Prophet" has Statue Made for Antichrist after an Assassination Attempt

This exalted religious figure, the false prophet (post-raptured Pope), will "deceive them that dwell on the earth by the means of those miracles which he had power to do in the sight of the beast [the Anti-Semite / Antichrist]; saying to them that dwell on earth, **that they should make an image to the beast** [the Anti-Semite / Antichrist], which had the wound by a sword, and did live." (Revelation 13:14)

✓ The "false prophet" who will occupy the position of Pope in the post-raptured church will be able to perform signs and wonders on behalf of the beast (Antichrist). This false prophet (post-raptured Pope) will deceive the inhabitants of the earth by ordering the world to set up an image in honor of the beast (the greatest Anti-Semite) who was wounded by the sword and yet lived.

✓ Since most European nations, composed of an educated populous, will have been destroyed, it will not be difficult for these two leaders to have poor third world nations follow their economic and religious reforms.

Prophecy No. 60

False Prophet Commands All Nations to Worship the Statue of the Anti-Semite/Antichrist or be Executed

This (post-raptured Pope) "false prophet" from the post-raptured Catholic (Universal) Church will have "power to give life unto the image of the beast, that the image of the beast should both speak, and cause that as many as would not worship the image of the beast [the Anti-Semite / Antichrist's statue] should be killed." (Revelation 13:15)

Prophecy No. 61

The False Prophet Mandates All Pledge Allegiance to the Anti-Semite/Antichrist by Taking the "Mark"

The post-raptured Pope that the Scriptures refers to as "the false prophet" of the post-raptured Catholic Church will draft a policy that "causeth all, both small and great, rich and poor, free and bond, to receive a mark in their right hand, or in their foreheads: and that no man might buy or sell, save he that had the mark, or the name of the beast [the Anti-Semite / Antichrist], or the number of his name.... Let him that hath understanding count the number of the beast [the Anti-Semite / Antichrist]: for it is the name of a man; and his number is Six hundred (600) three score (3 x 20 = 60) and six (666)." (Revelation 13:16-17)

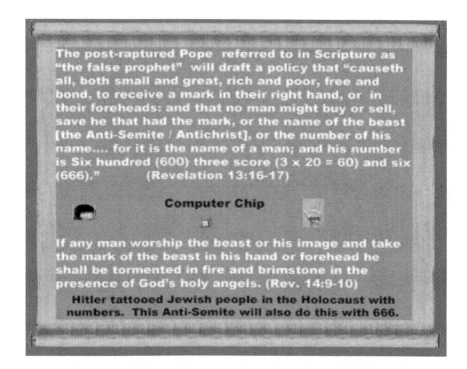

The post-raptured Pope referred to in Scripture as "the false prophet" will draft a policy that "causeth all, both small and great, rich and poor, free and bond, to receive a mark in their right hand, or in their foreheads: and that no man might buy or sell, save he that had the mark, or the name of the beast [the Anti-Semite / Antichrist], or the number of his name.... for it is the name of a man; and his number is Six hundred (600) three score (3 x 20 = 60) and six (666)." (Revelation 13:16-17)

Computer Chip

If any man worship the beast or his image and take the mark of the beast in his hand or forehead he shall be tormented in fire and brimstone in the presence of God's holy angels. (Rev. 14:9-10)

Hitler tattooed Jewish people in the Holocaust with numbers. This Anti-Semite will also do this with 666.

✓ The Mark of the Beast, 666, or the name of the beast in the palm of one's hand or foreheads makes one *eligible* to be able to participate in the world's economic system. (Rev. 13:16-18)

✓ If a person takes the Mark of the Beast, the Anti-Semite / Antichrist's name, or 666 in one's right hand or forehead that person is *ineligible* to enter the kingdom of heaven, period.

✓ Tattooing is ever popular; so many people will not think it strange to receive a mark of 666 in their palm or forehead. Whether the mark will be a scar from an implanted chip or a bar code on ones skin is unknown.

Prophecy No. 62
Jerusalem Surrounded by Armies: Enemies Rejoice

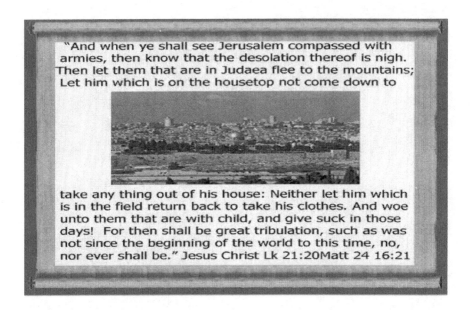

"And when ye shall see Jerusalem compassed with armies, then know that the desolation thereof is nigh. Then let them that are in Judaea flee to the mountains; Let him which is on the housetop not come down to take any thing out of his house: Neither let him which is in the field return back to take his clothes. And woe unto them that are with child, and give suck in those days! For then shall be great tribulation, such as was not since the beginning of the world to this time, no, nor ever shall be." Jesus Christ Lk 21:20Matt 24 16:21

"All that pass by clap their hands at thee; they hiss and wag their head at the daughter of Jerusalem [the Jews], saying, Is this the city that men call The perfection of beauty, The joy of the whole earth? All thine enemies have opened their mouth against thee: they hiss and gnash the teeth: they say, We have swallowed her up: certainly this is the day that we looked for; we have found, we have seen it." (Jeremiah's Lamentations 2:15-16)

✓ Arab nations will rejoice at the despair of the nation of Israel, when they see her on the brink of destruction, the day they dreamed of her annihilation.

Prophecy No. 63
Jews Flee Jerusalem when Antichrist Invades their Yet-to-be built Jewish Temple on the Temple Mount

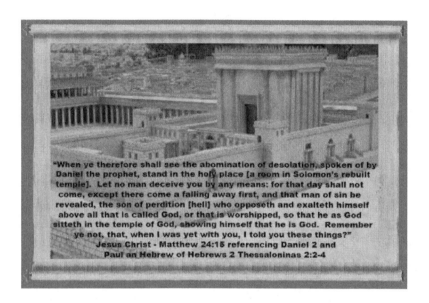

"When ye therefore shall see the abomination of desolation, spoken of by Daniel the prophet, stand in the holy place [a room in Solomon's rebuilt temple]. Let no man deceive you by any means: for that day shall not come, except there come a falling away first, and that man of sin be revealed, the son of perdition [hell] who opposeth and exalteth himself above all that is called God, or that is worshipped, so that he as God sitteth in the temple of God, showing himself that he is God. Remember ye not, that, when I was yet with you, I told you these things?"
Jesus Christ - Matthew 24:15 referencing Daniel 2 and
Paul an Hebrew of Hebrews 2 Thessaloninas 2:2-4

"When ye therefore shall see the abomination of desolation [the Anti-Semite/Antichrist], spoken of by Daniel the prophet, stand in the holy place [of Solomon's rebuilt temple]. Then let them which be in Judea [Israel] flee into the mountains: Let him which is on the housetop not come down to take any thing out of his house: Neither let him which is in the field return back to take his clothes. And woe unto them that are with child, and to them that give suck in those days! But pray ye that your flight [fleeing away] be not in the winter neither on the Sabbath day [Orthodox Jews do not work on the Sabbath]: For then shall be <u>great</u> <u>tribulation,</u> such as was not since the beginning of the world to this time, no, nor ever shall be. And except those days should be shortened [by His 2ⁿᵈ Coming], there should no flesh be saved: but for the elect's sake those days shall be shortened. Then if any man shall say unto you, Lo, here is Christ, or there; believe it not. For **there shall arise false Christs, and false prophets, and shall show great signs and wonders; insomuch that, if it were possible, they shall deceive the very elect**. Behold, I have told you before. Wherefore if they say unto you, Behold he is in the desert; go not forth: behold, he is in the secret chambers; believe it not. For as the lighting cometh out of the east, and shineth even unto the west; so shall also the coming of the Son of man be." (Jesus Christ: Matthew 24:15-27)

✓ Jesus Christ warned future generations of this global leader's invasion of their Jewish temple in Jerusalem.

✓ Here Christ is referring to Daniel's prophecy of the desecration of Jerusalem's temple when the Anti-Semite / Antichrist confiscates and occupies the rebuilt temple of Solomon, in Jerusalem, for 3½ years.

✓ The curious Christ seekers will be massacred for seeking Christ instead of being devoted to the Anti-Semite / Antichrist; therefore, Christ warns them not to go seeking for Him on earth. When Jesus Christ returns, the whole world will see Him. (Revelation 1:7)

Prophecy No. 64
The Anti-Semite/Antichrist Enters the Israelis' Temple Declaring that He is God

"Let no man deceive you by any means: for that day shall not come, except there come a falling away first, and that man of sin be revealed, the son of perdition [hell] who opposeth and exalteth himself above all that is called God, or that is worshipped, so that he as God sitteth in the temple of God, showing himself that he is God. Remember ye not, that, when I was yet with you, I told you these things? And now ye know what withholdeth [restrains] that he might be revealed in his time. And then shall that Wicked be revealed ... Even him, whose coming is after the working of Satan with all power and signs and lying wonders, And with all deceivableness of unrighteousness in them that perish; because they received not the love of the truth, that they might be saved. And for this cause God shall send them strong delusion [this mock resurrection, great signs, and wonders by the post raptured false prophet], that they should believe a lie: That they all might be damned who believe not the truth, but had pleasure in unrighteousness." (2 Thessalonians 2:3-12)

The love of the truth they reject is found in John 3:16 that: "God so loved the world, that he gave his only begotten Son, that whosoever believeth in him should not perish, but have everlasting life." (Jesus Christ: John 3:16)

✓ "I am come in my Father's name, and ye receive me not: if another shall come in his own name [the Beast / the Antichrist], him ye will receive." (Jesus Christ: John 5:43)

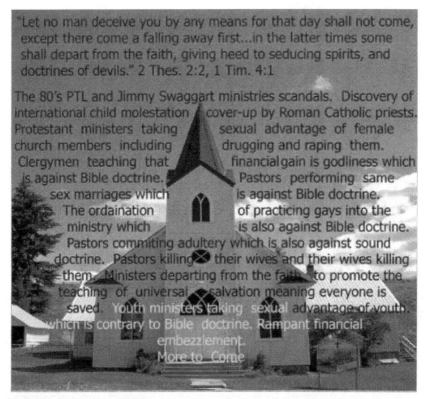

"Let no man deceive you by any means for that day shall not come, except there come a falling away first...in the latter times some shall depart from the faith, giving heed to seducing spirits, and doctrines of devils." 2 Thes. 2:2, 1 Tim. 4:1

The 80's PTL and Jimmy Swaggart ministries scandals. Discovery of international child molestation cover-up by Roman Catholic priests. Protestant ministers taking sexual advantage of female church members including drugging and raping them. Clergymen teaching that financial gain is godliness which is against Bible doctrine. Pastors performing same sex marriages which is against Bible doctrine. The ordination of practicing gays into the ministry which is also against Bible doctrine. Pastors commiting adultery which is also against sound doctrine. Pastors killing their wives and their wives killing them. Ministers departing from the faith to promote the teaching of universal salvation meaning everyone is saved. Youth ministers taking sexual advantage of youth, which is contrary to Bible doctrine. Rampant financial embezzlement.
More to Come

Prophecy No. 65
The Temple is Defiled by the Anti-Semite/Antichrist

"Yea, he magnified himself even to the prince of the host [Jesus the Christ], and by him the daily sacrifice was taken away, and the place of the sanctuary was cast down. And an host was given him against the daily sacrifice by reason of transgression, and it cast down the truth to the ground; and it practiced, and prospered. Then I heard one saint speaking, and another saint said unto that certain saint which spake, How long shall be the vision concerning the [temple's] daily sacrifice, and the transgression of desolation, to give both the sanctuary and the host to be trodden under foot? And he said unto me, Unto two thousand and three hundred days [3½ years]; then shall the sanctuary be cleansed [at the 2nd Coming of the Savior, Jesus Christ]"… "when he [Jesus Christ] will thoroughly purge his floor [the area called the court of the gentiles on which the Dome of the Rock, a holy Islamic mosque sits]." (Daniel 8:11-14, Matthew 3:12)

Prophecy No. 66
Antichrist Curses God After Declaring Himself God

The Anti-Semite/Antichrist "shall do according to his will; and he shall exalt himself, and magnify himself above every god, and shall speak marvelous things against the God of gods, and shall prosper till the indignation be accomplished: for that that is determined shall be done." (Daniel 11:36)

✓ The Anti-Semite/Antichrist's blasphemy toward the God of gods will resonate with people of the world who will hate God for bringing such harsh judgments upon the earth and allowing the nuclear war, famine, mass destruction, and pestilence on unbelieving men, women, and their children alike.

✓ Although Christians call him the Antichrist, the Bible states that he will magnify himself "above all that is called god," not just Jesus Christ and Allah, but idols too.

✓   We see America becoming more and more "anti-Christ" especially during the Christmas season. Traditional phrases such as Merry Christmas and Christmas Trees are being assaulted in overt attempts to expunge the name of "Christ" from American tradition. Traditional words such as Merry Christmas and Christmas Trees are being replaced by phrases like Happy Holidays, Season Greetings, and Xmas Trees indicative of a pro-antichrist atmosphere.   The age of antichrist sentiments is settling upon the nation who once worshipped "the God of Israel," the God of the Bible that is referred to on American currency.

In American history the United States' mantra was God and country. Yet, a telling sign of the times is displayed on the new millennium's American quarter with George Washington's back toward "In God We Trust" as his faces "Liberty." Soon the country's motto of "In God We Trust" will be expunged from American currency. A Psalmist wrote, "The wicked shall be turned into hell, and all nations that forget God." (Ps. 9:17) According to the Holy Scripture, we can see that America and other European nations that have also forgotten God are in for some hellish days ahead.

Prophecy No. 67
The Anti-Semite/Antichrist Curses the Raptured and Deceased Saints in Heaven

"And there was given unto him [the Anti-Semite / Antichrist] a mouth speaking great things and blasphemies; and power was given unto him to continue forty and two months [3 ½ years]. And he opened his mouth in blasphemy against God, to blaspheme his name, and his tabernacle, <u>and them that dwell in heaven</u> [raptured saints.]" (Revelation 13:5-6)

Prophecy No. 68
Antichrist Turn Anti-Semite and Declares War on Saints

"And it was given him [the Anti-Semite global ruler known as Antichrist] to make war with the saints, and to overcome them: and power was given him over all kindreds, and tongues, and nations. And all that dwell upon the earth shall worship him, whose names are not written in the book of life of the Lamb [Jesus] slain from the foundation of the world." (Revelation 13:7-8)

✓ The definition of saints according to the Scriptures differs considerably from whom the Roman Catholic Church qualifies as saints. According to Catholic tradition a person must be dead and then the Church of Rome must deem that person has performed a miracle in his or her lifetime and then that person is voted to become a saint. However, according to Scripture whosoever by faith accepts Jesus Christ as savior is counted as sanctified, holy, and declared righteous based on the merits of Jesus Christ's death, blood, and resurrection for their souls' salvation. Hence, they are declared "set apart," i.e., sanctified or a *saint* in the sight of God by the sacrifice of Jesus Christ and given the free gift of eternal redemption, eternal salvation, and eternal life, on the basis on what Christ did for them, and not what they did or do for Him (works). Salvation is a "free gift."

Prophecy No. 69
Antichrist Blasphemes God and Crushes Believers
"And he shall speak great words against the most High, and shall wear out the saints [believers in Christ during the Great Tribulation Period]." (Daniel 7:25)

Prophecy No. 70
The Anti-Semite/Antichrist Will be Revered
"And they worshipped the dragon [Satan] which gave power to the beast [Anti-Semite/Antichrist]: and they worshipped the beast [Anti-Semite/Antichrist]: saying, Who is like unto the beast? Who is able to make war with him?" (Revelation 13:4)

Prophecy No. 71
The Anti-Semite/Antichrist Goes Forth to Conquer
"He shall enter the glorious land and many countries shall be overthrown: but these shall escape out of his hand, even Edom, and Moab, and the chief of the children of Ammon [the Jordanians]." (Daniel 11:41)

Prophecy No. 72
Russia Wars Against the Anti-Semite/Antichrist

"...He shall divide the land for gain [a price]. And at the time of the end shall the king of the South push at him and the king of the north [Russia] shall come against him like a whirlwind, with chariots, and with horsemen, and with many ships; and he shall enter into the countries, and shall overflow and pass over." (Daniel 11:39-40)

Prophecy No. 73
The Anti-Semite/AntichristDevastates Egypt

"He shall stretch forth his hand also upon the countries and the land of Egypt shall not escape." (Daniel 11:42)

✓ Egypt will be so decimated that neither man nor beast will be able to walk across its land for 40 years. (Ezekiel 29:10-11)

Prophecy No. 74
Antichrist Enjoys Spoils of War and Practices Wealth Redistribution and the World Loves Him

"But he shall have power over the treasures of gold and silver, and over all the precious things of Egypt: and the Libyans and the Ethiopians shall be at his steps." (Daniel 11:43)

"He shall enter peaceably even upon the fattest places of the province; and **he shall do that which his fathers have not done, nor his fathers' fathers; he shall scatter among them the prey, and spoil, and riches:** yea, and he shall forecast his devices against the strong holds, even for a time." (Daniel 11:24)

Prophecy No. 75
The Peace Covenant With Israel is Broken
The Anti-Semite/Antichrist attacks Israel, "He hath put forth his hands against such as be at peace with him: <u>he hath broken his covenant.</u> □"The words of his mouth were smoother than butter, but war was in his heart: his words were softer than oil, yet were they drawn swords." (Psalms 55:20-21)

Prophecy No. 76
Jerusalem Is Invaded
"The kings of the earth, and all the inhabitants of the world, would not have believed that the adversary and the enemy should have entered into the gates of Jerusalem." (Lamentations 4:12)

✓   According to Jewish prophets, God will bring "such evil" on Jerusalem in this "the time of Jacob's [Israel's] trouble."

"And the Lord spake by his prophets saying…, thus saith the Lord God of Israel, Behold, I am bringing such evil upon Jerusalem and Judah, that whosoever heareth of it, both of his ears will tingle….and I will forsake the remnant of mine inheritance [the nation of Israel] and deliver them into the hands of their enemies, Because they have done that which was evil in my sight, and have provoked me to anger, since the day their fathers came out of the land of Egypt, even until this day." (2 Kings 21:16)

✓ In Jerusalem, the Israelites begged to shed the blood of an innocent man, the Son of God, of whom Pilate asked, "Why, what evil hath he done? But they cried out the more, saying, Let him be crucified. When Pilate saw that he could prevail nothing, but that rather a tumult was made, he took water, and washed his hands before the multitude, saying, I am innocent of the blood of this just person: see ye to it. Then answered all the people, and said, His blood be on us, and on our children." (Matthew 27:23-25)

Prophecy No. 77
A Divided Jerusalem to be Plundered

"For I will gather all nations against Jerusalem to battle; and the city shall be taken, and the houses rifled, and the women ravished; and <u>half of the city</u> shall go forth into captivity, and the residue of the people shall not be cut off from the city." (Zechariah 14:2)

"and the holy city [Jerusalem] shall they tread under foot forty and two months [3 ½ years]." (Revelation 11:2)

✓ Recent U.S. Presidents from Clinton, Bush, and Obama want plans in the works to divide Jerusalem in half. This will eventually happen and ultimately result in this prophecy being fulfilled in that the Jewish "half of the city will go into captivity" with its "houses rifled and the women ravished," according to the Jewish prophet Zechariah.

Prophecy No. 78
Antichrist's Siege of Jerusalem Causes Man-Made Famine Spawning Cannibalism Within Her Gates

"But woe unto them that are with child, and to them that give suck, in those days! For there shall be great distress in the land, and wrath upon this people." (Luke 21:23)

"And thou shalt eat the fruit of thine own body, the flesh of thy sons and of thy daughters, which the LORD thy God hath given thee, in the siege, and in the straitness, wherewith thine enemies shall distress thee: So that the man that is tender among you, and very delicate, his eye shall be evil toward his brother, and toward the wife of his bosom, and toward the remnant of his children which he shall leave: So that he will not give to any of them of the flesh of his children whom he shall eat: because he hath nothing left him in the siege, and in the straitness, wherewith thine enemies shall distress thee in all thy gates." (Deuteronomy 28:53-55)

"Yea, all Israel have transgressed thy law, even by departing, that they might not obey thy voice; therefore the curse is poured upon us, and the oath that is written in the law of Moses the servant of God, because we have sinned against him. And he hath confirmed his words, which he spake against us, and against our judges that judged us, by bringing upon us a great evil: for under the whole heaven hath not been done as hath been done upon Jerusalem. <u>As it is written in the law of Moses, all this evil is come upon us</u>: yet made we not our prayer before the LORD our God, that we might turn from our iniquities, and understand thy truth. Therefore hath the LORD watched upon the evil, and brought it upon us: for the LORD our God is righteous in all his works which he doeth: for we obeyed not his voice." (Daniel 9: 11-14)

✓ After this temple invasion, no food will be allowed in the Jewish half of Jerusalem causing a localized famine of barbaric proportions there.

✓ Per Moses' prophecy, those in the city of Jerusalem shall eat their young in the siege.

✓ "The tender and delicate woman among you, which would not adventure to set the sole of her foot upon the ground for delicateness and tenderness, her eye shall be evil toward the husband of her bosom, and toward her son, and toward her daughter, And toward her young one that cometh out from between her feet, and toward her children which she shall bear: for she shall eat them for want of all things secretly in the siege and straitness, wherewith thine enemy shall distress thee in thy gates." (Deuteronomy 28:56-57)

Prophecy No. 79
2/3 of Jews massacred by Anti-Semite/ Antichrist, as Israel Looks for America to Save Her 1/3 of the Jews in Israel will survive

"And it shall come to pass, that in all the land, saith the LORD, **two parts therein shall be cut off and die**; but the third shall be left therein. And **I will bring the third part through the fire**, and will refine them as silver is refined, and will try them as gold is tried: they shall call on my name, and I will hear them: I will say, It is my people: and they shall say, The LORD is my God." (Zechariah 13 :8-9)

✓ "Who is able to make war against the beast [Anti-Semite/ Antichrist]?" (Revelation 13:4)

"They that be slain with the sword are better than they that be slain with hunger: for these pine away, stricken through for want of the fruits of the field.... As for us, our eyes as yet failed for our vain help: **in our watching we have watched for a nation that could not save us.** They hunt our steps, that we cannot go in our streets: our end is near, our days are fulfilled; for our end is come. Our persecutors are swifter than the eagles of the heaven: they pursued us upon the mountains, they laid wait for us in the wilderness." (Jeremiah's Lamentations 4:9, 17-19)

Though many Africans have starved to death it has not reduced them to cannibalism. When Jerusalem is surrounded by the Anti-Semite / Antichrist's armies in siege, Moses wrote: "Because of the suffering that your enemy will inflict on you during the siege, you will eat the fruit of the womb, the flesh of the sons and daughters the LORD has given you. The most gentle and sensitive man among you will have no compassion on his own brother or wife he loves or his surviving children, and he will not give to one of them any of the flesh of his children that he is eating. It will be all he has left in the siege his enemies shall inflict upon your cities." (Deuteronomy 8:53-55) "Israel did not obey God therefore the curse is poured out on them written in the law of Moses. by bringing upon Jerusalem a great evil under heaven written by Moses." (Daniel 9:11-14)

Prophecy No. 80
World Astonished Israel Invaded & Jerusalem Sieged
"The hands of the pitiful women have sodden [boiled] their own children: they were their meat in the destruction of the daughter of my people. The LORD hath accomplished his fury; he hath poured out his fierce anger, and hath kindled a fire in Zion, and it hath devoured the foundations thereof. The kings of the earth, and all the inhabitants of the world, would not have believed that the adversary and the enemy should have entered into the gates of Jerusalem." (The weeping prophet of Israel's Lamentations 4:10-12)

✓ This is why "Jesus wept" over Jerusalem because He understood the prophecy that if the Israelis rejected Him as the Son of God, the Messiah of Israel, then according to their own prophets, the judgment of God for rejecting His Son would be that they would eat their own sons and daughters in the last days called the time of Jacob's trouble. (Jer. 30:7)

Prophecy No. 81
The Anti-Semite Antichrist/Antimessiah is Called a Destroyer of the Gentiles (KJV Term For Europeans)
"and the destroyer of the Gentiles is on his way; he is gone forth from his place to make thy land desolate; and thy cities shall be laid waste, without an inhabitant." (Jeremiah 4:7)

✓ Before the resurrection of Jesus Christ, when the term Gentile was used in Scripture, it was always used in reference to Europeans.

✓ Moses referred to the descendants of Japheth, the father of the Caucasians as "the Gentiles." (Genesis 10:2-5)

✓ Christ referenced Europeans of Rome as "the Gentiles." (Mark 10:33)

✓ Paul the "Apostle to the Gentiles" preached exclusively to the Europeans. (Romans 11:13)

✓ The time prior to the rise of the Anti-Semite/Antichrist is referred to in Scripture as *the times of the gentiles*," the era of European influence dominating world rule. (Luke 21:24)

✓ The only way cities of Europe will be "laid waste" without one inhabitant will be due to nuclear war.

Prophecy No. 82
144,000 Jewish Men Ordained by God to Preach the Gospel of the Kingdom During the Great Tribulation
"Saying, Hurt not the earth, neither the sea, nor the trees, till we have sealed the servants of our God in their foreheads. ☐And I heard the number of them which were sealed: and there were sealed an hundred and forty and four thousand of all the tribes of the children of Israel. Of the tribe of Judah were sealed twelve thousand. Of the tribe of Reuben were sealed twelve thousand...." (Revelation 7:3-8)

✓ After believers in Christ for His eternal salvation are *raptured* from earth (see Prophecy No. 150), their gospel of the grace of God "to believe on the Lord Jesus Christ to be saved" will no longer be preached. According to John the Revelator, an angel will seal 144,000 virgin Jewish men, 12,000 from each of the allegedly lost twelve tribes of Israel to preach the gospel that John the Baptist preached, *"the gospel of the kingdom."* (Revelation 7:2-8)

✓ Unlike *the gospel of the grace of God* which states, "Believe on the Lord Jesus Christ and you will be saved," the message of *the gospel of the kingdom* is; "behold the Lamb of God that taketh away the sin of the world. Jesus who is called the Lamb is coming, make straight paths for his feet. Do not take the mark of the beast or the number of his name or his name in your palm or forehead, prepare your hearts for the coming of the Lord draweth nigh."

Prophecy No. 83
Gospel Preached to World then shall The End Come
"And this *gospel of the kingdom* will be preached in the whole world as a testimony to all nations, and then the end will come." (Matthew. 24:14)

✓ "The end" culminates with the saints coming back with Jesus Christ at his Second Coming. Therefore, these saints will not be the ones preaching the gospel of the kingdom to all the earth. The gospel of the kingdom will be preached throughout

the world by 144,000 sealed virgin Jewish men, who will be converted *after* the church is taken out of this world in what is known in Jewish Scripture as "the blessed hope" or "a mystery" but called *the rapture* of the church by gentile theologians, and then shall the end come.

Prophecy No. 84

God Commissions Two Witnesses to Earth

God will send two men to earth and they shall curse with plagues those with the mark of the beast, the beast's name, or 666 in their hand or forehead. John writes: "And I will give power unto my two witnesses, and they shall prophesy a thousand two hundred and threescore days [3½ years], clothed in sackcloth [black]… And if any man will hurt them, fire proceedeth out of their mouth, and devoureth their enemies: and if any man will hurt them, he must in this manner be killed. These have power to shut heaven, that it rain not in the days of their prophecy: and have power over waters to turn them to blood, and to smite the earth with all plagues, as often as they will.

"And when they shall have finished their testimony, the beast [the Anti-Semite/Antichrist] … shall make war against them, and shall overcome them, and kill them." (Revelation 11:3-7)

✓ Isn't it ironic that with all the sci-fi horror movies from Hollywood, not one film in the history of American cinema has attempted to dramatize the book of the Revelation and stay true to the Scriptures regarding the end times as recited in the Holy Scriptures and featured in this book.

Prophecy No. 85

World Media Covers the Deaths of the Two Witnesses

"And their dead bodies shall lie in the street of the great city [Jerusalem], which spiritually is called Sodom and Egypt, where also our Lord was crucified. ☐And they of the people and kindreds and tongues and **nations shall see their dead bodies** [possible by mass media] three days and an half, and shall not suffer their dead bodies to be put in graves. ☐And they that dwell upon the earth shall rejoice over them, and make merry, and shall send gifts one to another; because these two prophets tormented them that dwelt on the earth. And after three days and an half the spirit of life from God entered into them, and they stood upon their feet; and great fear fell upon them which saw them. And they heard a great voice from heaven saying unto them, Come up hither. And they ascended up to heaven in a cloud; and their enemies beheld [saw] them." (Revelation 11:8-12)

✓ "And there was war in heaven: Michael and his angels fought against the dragon; and the dragon fought and his angels, …. And the great dragon was cast out, that old serpent, called the Devil, and Satan, which deceiveth the whole world: he was cast out into the earth, and his angels were cast out with him. Therefore rejoice, ye heavens, and ye that dwell in them… Woe to the inhibiters of the earth and of the sea! For the devil is come down unto you, having great wrath, because he knoweth that he hath but a short time." (Revelation 12:7-12)

"...great signs shall be from heaven. But before all these, they shall lay their hands on you, and persecute you, delivering you up to the synagogues, and into prisons, being brought before kings and rulers for my name's sake. And it shall turn to you for a testimony. Settle it therefore in your hearts, not to meditate before what ye shall answer: For I will give you a mouth and wisdom, which all your adversaries shall not be able to gainsay nor resist. ꛷And ye shall be betrayed both by parents, and brethren, and kinsfolks, and friends; and some of you shall they cause to be put to death. ꛷And ye shall be hated of all men for my name's sake." (Jesus Christ: Luke 21:11-17)

Prophecy No. 86
Believers Will Be Betrayed to the State by Family

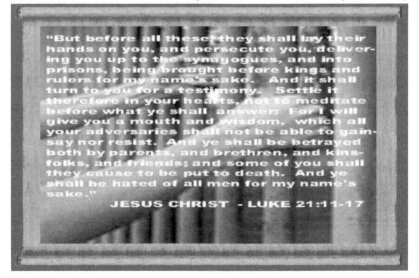

"But before all these, they shall lay their hands on you, and persecute you, delivering you up to the synagogues, and into prisons, being brought before kings and rulers for my name's sake. And it shall turn to you for a testimony. Settle it therefore in your hearts, not to meditate before what ye shall answer: For I will give you a mouth and wisdom, which all your adversaries shall not be able to gainsay nor resist. And ye shall be betrayed both by parents, and brethren, and kinsfolks, and friends; and some of you shall they cause to be put to death. And ye shall be hated of all men for my name's sake."
JESUS CHRIST - LUKE 21:11-17

Prophecy No. 87
Antichrist Will Behead Preachers of the Gospel of Christ's Return, the Gospel of the Kingdom

"And I saw thrones, and they sat upon them, and judgment was given unto them: and I saw the souls of them that were <u>beheaded for the witness of Jesus</u>, and for the word of God, and which had not worshipped the beast, neither his image, neither had received his mark upon their foreheads, or in their hands; and they lived and reigned with Christ a thousand years." (Revelation. 20:4)

Prophecy No. 88
Antichrist Makes War Against God's Saints

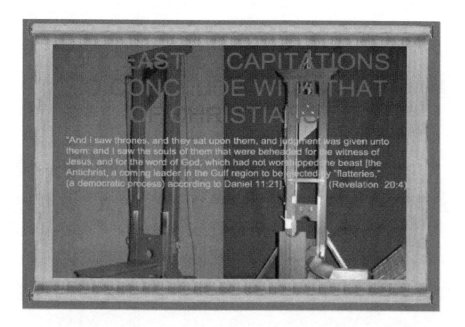

The Anti-Semite/Antichrist, called the beast, and the little horn "made war with the saints and prevailed against them." (Daniel 7:21)

Prophecy No. 89
God Avenges His Martyred Saints

"And the third angel poured out his vial upon the rivers and fountains of waters; and they became blood. And I heard the angel of the waters say, Thou art righteous, O Lord, which art, and wast, and shalt be, because thou hast judged thus. For they have shed the blood of saints and prophets, and thou hast given them blood to drink; for they are worthy. And I heard another out of the altar say, Even so, Lord God Almighty, true and righteous are thy judgments." (Revelation 16:4-7)

Prophecy No. 90
Martyred Saints Receive White Robes From God

"...I saw under the altar [in heaven] the souls of them that were slain for the word of God, and for the testimony which they held: And they cried with a loud voice, saying, How long, O Lord, holy and true, dost thou not judge and avenge our blood on them that dwell on the earth? And white robes were given unto every one of them; and it was said unto them, that they should rest yet for a little season, until their fellow servants also and their brethren, that should be killed as they were, should be fulfilled." (Revelation 6:9-11)

✓   The souls that will not submit to the reign of the Anti-Semite/Antichrist in favor of Jesus Christ will be slain, by edict of the Anti-Semite/Antichrist, during the Great Tribulation which will be the last 3½ years of this Anti-Semite's seven year reign as ruler of the head (superpower) of all nations. Now, salvation is free just by placing one's faith in Jesus' death, blood, and resurrection for life everlasting coupled with the eternal forgiveness of sins. However, after the believers are taken out of this world, so this wicked one can be revealed, those who then choose to accept Jesus Christ as their salvation will pay for that decision, made under the reign of the Anti-Semite/Antichrist, with their lives. "Believe on the Lord Jesus Christ and thou shalt be saved."

Prophecy No. 91
Post-Raptured Catholic Church of Rome Is Judged
"Come hither; and I will show unto thee the judgment of the great whore that sitteth on many waters. With whom the kings of the earth have committed fornication, [she has had political influence with kings] and the inhabitants of the earth have been made drunk with the wine of her fornication [false doctrines]. And I saw the woman drunken with the blood of the saints, and with the blood of the martyrs of Jesus: [through inquisitions in the name of Christianity]…Here is the mind which hath wisdom. The seven heads are the seven mountains on which the woman sits. And the woman which thou sawest is that great city, which reigned over the kings of the earth."
(Revelation. 17:2-18)

✓   The church that believes in God and His Son Jesus Christ alone, for their soul's salvation is called the bride of Christ, a chaste virgin, whereas the false church that has political influence with kings and governments on the earth and has killed the saints in the name of Christianity is referenced to by St. John the Apostle "Mystery Babylon the Great Whore" according to Revelation 17:5-6. Furthermore, the Scripture above reveals her location is situated as a queen on the seven hills in Rome.   Many born again Christians are in this church preaching the gospel of salvation through Jesus Christ.

✓   During the Middle Ages the Catholic Church in Rome, that sits on *"seven mountains,"* exercised great authority with and over the kings of the earth, whether it was by her Cardinals in France or her priests in Great Britain and elsewhere. Here God is bringing judgment on her for the blood of those martyrs that she shed in her earlier inquisitions. Today she is a shadow of her former self, but she shall rise in world prominence again.

✓   John's prophecy takes place after believers in Christ for salvation, including those in the Catholic Church, have been raptured out of this world. (See Prophecy No. 150). In John's vision, he explains how God will have the Anti-Semite / Antichrist handle this post-raptured false church when its false prophet, the post rapture Pope, reigns from there and will turn the hearts of those who missed the rapture with him from seeking Jesus, to the worship of the Antichrist.

John wrote, "And I saw the woman drunken with the blood of the saints, and with the blood of the martyrs of Jesus [by its inquisitions]: ... And he saith unto me, The waters which thou sawest, where the whore sitteth, are peoples, and multitudes, and nations, and tongues. And the ten horns [Ten Middle Eastern kings] which thou sawest upon the beast, these shall hate the whore [post-raptured false church], and shall make her desolate and naked, and shall eat her flesh, and burn her with fire. **For God hath put in their hearts to fulfill his will, and to agree, and give their kingdom unto the beast [Anti-Semite / Antichrist], until the words of God shall be fulfilled.** And the woman which thou sawest is that great city, which reigneth over the kings of the earth. And I heard another voice from heaven, saying, **Come out of her, my people, that ye be not partakers of her sins, and that ye receive not of her plagues. For her sins have reached unto heaven, and God hath remembered her iniquities."** (Revelation 17:6 – 18:5)

Prophecy No. 92
The Anti-Semite/Antichrist Destroys Vatican City

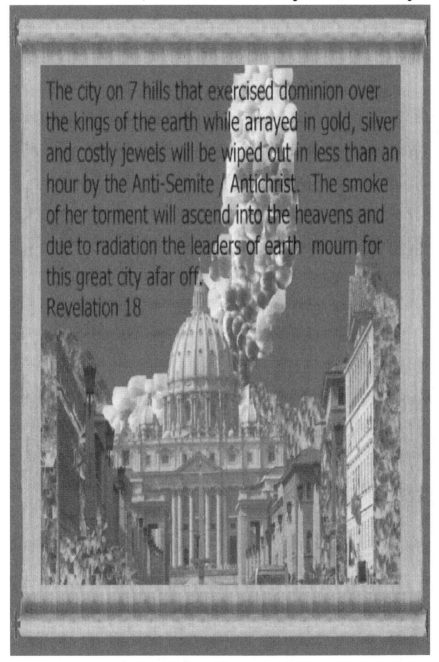

The city on 7 hills that exercised dominion over the kings of the earth while arrayed in gold, silver and costly jewels will be wiped out in less than an hour by the Anti-Semite / Antichrist. The smoke of her torment will ascend into the heavens and due to radiation the leaders of earth mourn for this great city afar off.
Revelation 18

Rome to be Destroyed by the Antichrist

"And I heard another voice from heaven, saying, Come out of her, my people, that ye be not partakers of her sins, and that ye receive not of her plagues. For her sins have reached unto heaven, and God hath remembered her iniquities...Therefore shall her plagues come in one day, death, and mourning, and famine; and she shall be utterly burned with fire: for strong is the Lord God who judgeth her. And the kings of the earth, who have committed fornication and lived deliciously with her, shall bewail her, and lament for her, when they shall see the smoke of her burning, Standing afar off for the fear of her torment, saying, Alas, alas that great city Babylon, that mighty city! For in one hour is thy judgment come. And the merchants of the earth shall weep and mourn over her; for no man buyeth their merchandise any more...The merchants of these things, which were made rich by her, shall stand afar off for the fear of her torment, weeping and wailing, And saying, Alas, alas that great city, that was clothed in fine linen, and purple, and scarlet, and decked with gold, and precious stones, and pearls! For in one hour so great riches is come to nought. And every shipmaster, and all the company in ships, and sailors, and as many as trade by sea, stood afar off, And cried when they saw the smoke of her burning, saying, What city is like unto this great city! And they cast dust on their heads, and cried, weeping and wailing, saying, Alas, alas that great city, wherein were made rich all that had ships in the sea by reason of her costliness! For in one hour is she made desolate. Rejoice over her, thou heaven, and ye holy apostles and prophets; for God hath avenged you on her... And the light of a candle shall shine no more at all in thee; and the voice of the bridegroom and of the bride shall be heard no more at all in thee: for thy merchants were the great men of the earth; for by thy sorceries were all nations deceived. <u>And in her was found the blood of prophets, and of saints,</u> and of all that were slain upon the earth." (Revelation 18:4-24)

✓ The Church of Rome has amassed such wealth that after the Anti-Semite / Antichrist declares himself God, he will demand this post-raptured Church to turn its wealth over to him and worship him, but she will refuse. Then the Anti-Semite / Antichrist, a Middle Easterner, will destroy this perceived post-raptured bastion of Christianity. According to the Apostle John, God will allow the Anti-Semite / Antichrist to execute his judgment on the Church of Rome and it will be blown off the map in less than an hour, according to Revelation 18:10. Today she is known as Vatican City.

✓ Due to nuclear radiation, all the merchants and kings of the earth will see "the smoke of her burning" will stand "afar off" lamenting her destruction.

Prophecy No. 93
The Stage is Set For the Great Battle of Armageddon
"And I saw an angel standing in the sun; and he cried with a loud voice, saying to all the fowls that fly in the midst of heaven, Come and gather yourselves together unto the supper of the great God; That ye may eat the flesh of kings, and the flesh of captains, and the flesh of mighty men, and the flesh of horses, and of them that sit on them, and the flesh of all men, both free and bond, both small and great." (Revelation 19:17-18)

Section Seven: The Coming of the Lord

Prophecy No. 94
The Lord Assembles His Army to Invade Earth

"Blow ye the trumpet in Zion, and sound an alarm in my holy mountain: let all the inhabitants of the land tremble: for the day of the LORD cometh, for it is nigh at hand; A day of darkness and of gloominess, a day of clouds and of thick darkness, as the morning spread upon the mountains: a great people and a strong; there hath not been ever the like, neither shall be any more after it, even to the years of many generations. A fire devoureth before them; and behind them a flame burneth: the land is as the garden of Eden before them, and behind them a desolate wilderness; yea, and nothing shall escape them. The appearance of them is as the appearance of horses; and as horsemen, so shall they run." (Joel 2:1-4)

Prophecy No. 95
Jesus Christ Returns

"And I saw heaven opened, and behold a white horse; and he that sat upon him was called Faithful and True, and in righteousness he doth judge and make war. His eyes were as a flame of fire, and on his head were many crowns; and he had a name written, that no man knew, but he himself. And he was clothed with a vesture dipped in blood: and his name is called The Word of God." (Revelation 19:11-13)

"In the beginning was the Word and the Word was with God and the <u>Word was God</u>. And the Word was made flesh and dwelt among us...he was in the world and the world was made by him and the world knew him not." (John 1:1,14,10)

Prophecy No. 96
The Second Coming of Jesus Christ
"And the armies which were in heaven followed him upon white horses, clothed in fine linen, white and clean. And he hath on his vesture and on his thigh a name written, KING OF KINGS, AND LORD OF LORDS." (Revelation 19:14-16)

Prophecy No. 97
The Earth Laments Christ's Return
"Behold he cometh with clouds; and every eye shall see him, and they also which pierced him: and all kindreds of the earth shall wail because of him. Even so, Amen." (Revelation 1:7)

Prophecy No. 98
All Tribes of the Earth Mourn Christ's Return
"And then shall appear the sign of the Son of man in heaven: ...and then shall all the tribes of the earth mourn, and they shall see the Son of Man coming in the clouds of heaven with power and great glory." (Matthew 24:30, Revelation 18:4-24)

"Behold, he cometh with clouds; and every eye shall see him, and they also which pierced him: and all kindreds of the earth shall wail because of him. Even so, Amen." (Rev. 1:7)

✓ The fulfillment of the prophecy of Christ's return was mentioned at His ascension into heaven on a cloud when men dressed in white said, "Ye men of Galilee, why stand ye

gazing up into heaven? This same Jesus, which is taken up from you into heaven, shall so come in like manner as ye have seen him go into heaven." (Acts 1:9-11)

Prophecy No. 99
Every Eye On Earth Shall See His Second Coming

"For as the lightning cometh out of the east, and shineth even unto the west; so shall also the coming of the Son of man be, and every eye shall see him." (Matthew 24:27, Revelation 1:7)

Prophecy No. 100
Kings of Earth Make War Against Christ at His Return

"And I saw the beast [the Anti-Semite / Antichrist], and the kings of the earth, and their armies, gathered together to make war against him that sat on the horse, and against his army [born again believers]." (Revelation 19:19)

Prophecy No. 101
The Lord Takes Vengeance on Unbelievers

"...the Lord Jesus shall be revealed from heaven with his mighty angels, In flaming fire taking vengeance on them that know not God, and that obey not the gospel of our Lord Jesus

Christ [to believe in Him for salvation]. Who shall be punished with everlasting destruction from the presence of the Lord, and from the glory of his power; When he shall come to be glorified in his saints, and to be admired in all them that believe in that day." (2 Thessalonians 1:7-10)

Prophecy No. 102
Battle of Armageddon: Christ Massacres Armies

"...hearken, ye people: let the earth hear, and all that is therein; the world, and all things that come forth of it. For the indignation of the LORD is upon all nations, and his fury upon all their armies: he hath utterly destroyed them, he hath delivered them to the slaughter. Their slain also shall be cast out, and their stink shall come up out of their carcasses, and the mountains shall be melted with their blood." (Isaiah 34:1-3)

Prophecy No. 103
Lord Fights for Jerusalem Destroying Their Enemies

"In that day shall the LORD defend the inhabitants of Jerusalem; and he that is feeble among them at that day shall be as David; and the house of David shall be as God, as the angel of the LORD before them.□ And it shall come to pass in that day, that I will seek to destroy all the nations that come against Jerusalem." (Zechariah 12:8-9)

"And this shall be the plague wherewith the LORD will smite all the people that have fought against Jerusalem; Their flesh shall consume away while they stand upon their feet [before they hit the ground], and their eyes shall consume away in their holes, and their tongue shall consume away in their mouth." (Zechariah 14:12)

Prophecy No. 105
The Lord Utters His Mighty Voice Before His Army,
and His Saints Execute Judgment

"Like the noise of chariots on the tops of mountains shall they leap, like the noise of a flame of fire that devoureth the stubble, as a strong people set in battle array.☐ Before their face the people shall be much pained: all faces shall gather blackness [happens to exposed skin after an atomic blast]. They shall run like mighty men; they shall climb the wall like men of war; and they shall march every one on his ways, and they shall not break their ranks: Neither shall one thrust another; they shall walk every one in his path: and when they fall upon the sword, they shall not be wounded.☐ They shall run to and fro in the city; they shall run upon the wall, they shall climb up upon the houses; they shall enter in at the windows like a thief. The earth shall quake before them; the heavens shall tremble: the sun and the moon shall be dark, and the stars shall withdraw their shining:☐ And the LORD shall utter his voice before his army: for his camp is very great: for he is strong that executeth his word: for the day of the LORD is great and very terrible; and who can abide it?" (Joel 2:5-11)

✓   Before Christ was crucified, He told Pilate that His kingdom was not of this world or else His servants would fight. (John 18:36) At His Second Coming, "when the kingdoms of this world become the kingdoms of the Lord and of his Christ," (Revelation 11:15) His servants [born again believers] will fight for Him.

"Let the saints be joyful in glory: let them sing aloud upon their beds. Let the high praises of God be in their mouth, and a two-edged sword in their hand; To execute vengeance upon the heathen, and punishments upon the people; To bind their kings with chains, and their nobles with fetters of iron; To execute upon them the judgment written: this honor have all his saints. Praise ye the LORD." (Psalm 149:5-9)

Prophecy No. 106
Jesus Christ Smites the Nations

"And the armies which were in heaven followed him upon white horses, clothed in fine linen, white and clean. And out of his mouth goeth a sharp sword, that with it he should smite the nations: and he shall rule them with a rod of iron: and he treadeth the winepress of the fierceness and wrath of Almighty God." (Revelation 19:14-15)

✓ We do not know what the fierceness and wrath of Almighty God is because He has restrained Himself from it during our New Testament era called grace. He has restrained Himself so much so that many of today's intelligentsia do not believe He exists.

Prophecy No. 107
Christ Slays the Armies Gathered at Armageddon

"And the armies which were in heaven followed him... And the remnant were slain with the sword of him that sat upon the horse, which sword proceeded out of his mouth: and all the fowls were filled with their flesh." (Revelation 19:14, 21)

Prophecy No. 108
Blood of 200 Million Men Slain by Christ produces
Blood Three Feet Deep Covering Over 100 Miles

"And the winepress was trodden without [outside] the city [Jerusalem], and blood came out of the winepress, even unto the horse bridles, by the space of a thousand and six hundred furlongs [137 miles]." (Revelation 14:20)

"I will leave thee upon the land, I will cast thee forth in the open field, and will cause the fowls of the heaven to remain upon thee, and I will fill the beasts of the whole earth with thee. I will lay thy flesh upon the mountains, and fill the valleys with thy height. I will also water with thy blood the land wherein thou swimmest, even to the mountains; and the rivers shall be full of thee." (Ezekiel 32:4-6)

Prophecy No. 109
Christ Puts Down Anti-Semite Antichrist & Waters
the Battlefield with the Blood of Earth's Armies

"And the beast [the Anti-Semite/Antichrist] was taken, and with him the false prophet [post-raptured Pope] that wrought miracles before him, with which he deceived them that had received the mark of the beast, and them that worshipped his image. These both were cast alive into a lake of fire burning with brimstone. And the remnant were slain with the sword of him that sat upon the horse, which sword proceeded out of his mouth: and all the fowls were filled with their flesh." (Revelation 19:20-21)

"And I will lay thy flesh upon the mountains, and fill the valleys with thy height. I will also water with thy blood the land wherein thou swimmest, even to the mountains; and the rivers shall be full of thee. And when I shall put thee out, I will cover the heaven, and make the stars thereof dark; I will cover the sun with a cloud, and the moon shall not give her light." (Ezekiel 32:5-7)

Prophecy No. 110
The Anti-Semite/Antichrist's Power is Broken
"I will break the Assyrian [the Anti-Semite/Antichrist] in my land [Israel's valley of Armageddon], and upon my mountains tread him under foot: then shall his yoke depart from off them, and his burden depart from off their shoulders. This is the purpose that is purposed upon the whole earth: ...upon all the nations. For the LORD of hosts hath purposed, and who shall disannul it? And his hand is stretched out, and who shall turn it back?" (Isaiah 14:25-27)

Section Eight: The Day of the Lord

Prophecy No. 111
The Kings of the Earth are Punished

"The earth shall reel to and fro like a drunkard, and shall be moved like a cottage; and the transgression thereof shall be heavy upon it; and it shall fall, and not rise again. And it shall come to pass in that day, that the LORD shall punish the host of the high ones that are on high, and the kings of the earth upon the earth. And they shall be gathered together, as prisoners are gathered in the pit, and shall be shut up in the prison [hell], and after many days shall they be visited [Judgment Day]. Then the moon shall be confounded, and the sun ashamed, when the LORD of hosts shall reign in mount Zion, and in Jerusalem, and before his ancients gloriously." (Isaiah 24:20-23)

Prophecy No. 112
The Day of the Lord

"The great day of the LORD is near, it is near, and hasteth greatly, even the voice of the day of the LORD: the mighty man shall cry there bitterly. That day is a day of wrath, a day of trouble and distress, a day of wastedness and destruction, a day of darkness and gloominess, a day of clouds and thick darkness." (Zephaniah 1:14-15)

Prophecy No. 113

Christ Reveals Wounds of His Crucifixion to Jewish Survivors of the Antichrist's Siege

"And one shall say unto him, What are these wounds in thine hands? Then he shall answer, Those with which I was wounded in the house of my friends." (Zechariah 13:6)

✓ This will be the moment when the Jews realize their forefathers did indeed crucify their Messiah, as foretold by King David, Goliath's slayer, and a Jewish prophet from the perspective of Messiah in the Psalm immediately prior to the 23rd Psalm of "The Lord is my shepherd in Psalm 22." (Psalm 23:1)

✓ "They pierced my hands and my feet." (King David's prophecy in first person) (Psalm 22:16, Luke 24:44)

Prophecy No. 114

Jewish Survivors of the Tribulation Mourn The Sins of Their Forefathers' Crucifixion of Jesus Christ

"...and they shall look upon me whom they have pierced, and they shall mourn for him, as one mourneth for his only son, and shall be in bitterness for him, as one that is in bitterness for his firstborn." (Zechariah 12:10)

Section Nine: Jesus Christ's Millennial Reign

Prophecy No. 115
Millennial (1,000 Year) Reign of Jesus Christ Begins

"And the seventh angel sounded; and there were great voices in heaven, saying, The kingdoms of this world are become the kingdoms of our Lord, and of his Christ; and he shall reign for ever and ever." (Revelation 11:15)

✓ Nostradamus also predicted this thousand years of peace after the Great War. Yet, John, the Jewish Revelator, foretold this long before Nostradamus and read John's Revelation. Secular society believes the predictions of Nostradamus and ignore and ridicule the prophecies of Scripture.

Prophecy No. 116
Satan Is Bound for a Thousand Years and Cast into the Bottomless Pit

"And He [Jesus Christ] laid hold on the dragon, that old serpent, which is the Devil, and Satan, and bound him a thousand years. And cast him into the bottomless pit, and shut him up, and set a seal upon him, that he should deceive the nations no more, till the thousand years should be fulfilled: and after that he must be loosed a little season. (Revelation 20:2-3

Prophecy No. 117

Satan Mocked By World Leaders Already in Hell as He Descends into Its Pit

"Hell from beneath is moved for thee to meet thee at thy coming: it stirreth up the dead for thee, even all the chief ones of the earth; it hath raised up from their thrones all the kings of the nations. All they shall speak and say unto thee, Art thou also become weak as we? Art thou become like unto us? □Thy pomp is brought down to the grave, and the noise of thy viols: the worm is spread under thee, and the worms cover thee. How art thou fallen from heaven, O Lucifer, son of the morning! How art thou cut down to the ground, which didst weaken the nations! .... Yet thou shalt be brought down to hell, to the sides of the pit. They that see thee shall narrowly look upon thee, and consider thee, saying, Is this the man that made the earth to tremble, that did shake kingdoms; That made the world as a wilderness, and destroyed the cities thereof; that opened not the house of his prisoners? All the kings of the nations, even all of them, lie in glory, every one in his own house. But thou art cast out of thy grave like an abominable branch, and as the raiment of those that are slain, thrust through with a sword, that go down to the stones of the pit; as a carcass trodden under feet. Thou shalt not be joined with them in burial, because thou hast destroyed thy land, and slain thy people: the seed of evildoers shall never be renowned." (Isaiah 14:9-20)

✓ Beware of the New International Version Bible's discourse in Isaiah 14:12. The NIV Bible removes Satan's name "Lucifer" and inserts the title of *morning star,* a title which belongs exclusive to Jesus Christ. Christ is known as "the bright and morning star." (Revelation 22:16) The NIV translation of this verse leans toward an interpretation that may lead people to believe that Christ weakened the nations.

Prophecy No. 118
Christ Establishes Jerusalem as World's Capitol
"At that time they shall call Jerusalem the throne of the LORD; and all the nations shall be gathered unto it, to the name of the LORD, to Jerusalem…" (Jeremiah 3:17)

Prophecy No. 119
Jerusalem Finally At Peace
The Lord will make Jerusalem live up to her name the city of Peace. "Whereas thou has been forsaken and hated, so that no man went through thee, I will make thee an eternal excellency, a joy of many generations. Thou shalt also suck the milk of the Gentiles, and shalt suck the breast of kings: and thou shalt know that I the LORD am thy Savior and thy Redeemer, the mighty One of Jacob. For brass I will bring gold, and for iron I will bring silver, and for wood brass, and for stones iron: I will also make thy officers peace, and thine exactors righteousness. Violence shall no more be heard in thy land, wasting nor destruction within thy borders; but thou shalt call thy walls Salvation, and thy gates Praise." (Isaiah 60:15-18)

Prophecy No. 120
The House of the Lord Shall Be Established

"But **in the last days** it shall come to pass, that the mountain of the house of the LORD shall be established in the top of the mountains, and it shall be exalted above the hills; and people shall flow unto it [the Temple Mount]. ☐And many nations shall come, and say, Come, and let us go up to the mountain of the LORD, and to the house of the God of Jacob; and he will teach us of his ways, and we will walk in his paths: for the law shall go forth of Zion, and the word of the LORD from Jerusalem. And he shall judge among many people, and rebuke strong nations afar off..."
(The Prophet Micah 4:1-4)

✓ "And I will execute great vengeance upon them with furious rebukes; and they shall know that I am the LORD, when I shall lay my vengeance upon them." (Ezekiel 25:17)

Prophecy No. 121
Christ Brings True Peace to the Middle East

In that day "...they shall beat their swords into plowshares, and their spears into pruning hooks: nation shall not lift up a sword against nation, neither shall they learn war any more. But they shall sit every man under his vine and under his fig tree; and none shall make them afraid: for the mouth of the LORD of hosts hath spoken it." (Micah 4:3-4)

Prophecy No. 122

A Highway Out of Egypt Is To Be Built

"In that day shall there be a highway out of Egypt to Assyria [Persian Region], and the Assyrian [the Persian] shall come into Egypt, and the Egyptian into Assyria, and the Egyptians shall serve with the Assyrians. In that day shall Israel be the third with Egypt and with Assyria, even a blessing in the midst of the land: Whom the LORD of hosts shall bless, saying, Blessed be Egypt my people, and Assyria the work of my hands, and Israel mine inheritance." (Isaiah 19:23-25)

Prophecy No. 123

Peace on Earth Lions Lay Down In Peace with Lambs

"The wolf also shall dwell with the lamb, and the leopard shall lie down with the kid; and the calf and the young lion and the fatling together; and a little child shall lead them.☐ And the cow and the bear shall feed; their young ones shall lie down together: and the lion shall eat straw like the ox.☐☐☐And the sucking child shall play on the hole of the asp, and the weaned child shall put his hand on the cockatrice' den. They shall not hurt nor destroy in all my holy mountain: for the earth shall be full of the knowledge of the LORD, as the waters cover the sea." (Isaiah 11:6-9)

Prophecy No. 124
Israel To Be Comforted By Her King

"Rejoice ye with Jerusalem, and be glad with her, all ye that love her: rejoice for joy with her, all ye that mourn for her: That ye may suck, and be satisfied with the breasts of her consolations; that ye may milk out, and be delighted with the abundance of her glory. For thus saith the LORD, Behold, I will extend peace to her like a river, and the glory of the Gentiles like a flowing stream: then shall ye suck, ye shall be borne upon her sides, and be dandled upon her knees. As one whom his mother comforteth, so will I comfort you; and ye shall be comforted in Jerusalem. ☐And when ye see this, your heart shall rejoice, and your bones shall flourish like an herb: and the hand of the LORD shall be known toward his servants, and his indignation toward his enemies." (Isaiah 66:10-14)

✓   Not everyone will like Christ during His 1000-year reign.

Prophecy No. 125
Christ Reigns In Jerusalem as King of Kings

"Of the increase of his government and peace there shall be no end, upon the throne of David, and upon his kingdom, to order it, and to establish it with judgment and with justice from henceforth even for ever. The zeal of the LORD of hosts will perform this…And in mercy shall the throne be established: and he shall sit upon it in truth in the tabernacle of David, judging, and seeking judgment, and hasting righteousness." (Isaiah 9:7, 16:5)

Prophecy No. 126
Christ's 12 Apostles Installed As Judges Over Israel
"Jesus said to his disciples, Verily I say unto you, ye which have followed me, in the regeneration when the Son of man shall sit in the throne of his glory, ye also shall sit upon twelve thrones, judging the twelve tribes of Israel." (Matthew 19:28)

Prophecy No. 127
Christ Annexes Much of Mid-East As New Israel To Fulfill God's Promise to His Chosen Hebrew People
"Every place whereon the soles of your feet shall tread shall be yours: from the wilderness and Lebanon, from the river, the river Euphrates, even unto the uttermost sea shall your coast be." (Deuteronomy 11:24)

The Land the Messiah of Israel Shall Annex As New Israel as Expected by Orthodox Jews

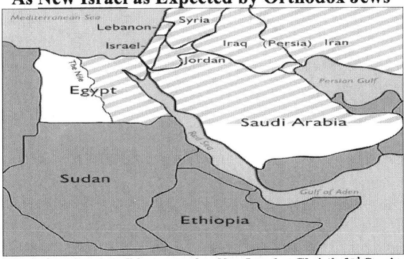

The Striped Land shall be annexed as <u>New Israel</u> at Christ's 2nd Coming
Egypt, Israel, Jordan, Saudi Arabia, Iraq (Ur), Iran, Syria, and Lebanon shall Compose New Israel

The Striped Shall be Annexed as New Israel at Christ's 2nd Coming. Egypt, Israel, Jordan, Iraq, Iran, Syria, Saudi Arabia, and Lebanon will comprise New Israel.

Prophecy No. 128
Nations to Send Delegates Annually to Jewish Feast
"And it shall be, that whoso will not come up of all the families of the earth unto Jerusalem to worship the King, the LORD of hosts, even upon them shall be no rain. And if the family of Egypt go not up, and come not, that have no rain; there shall be the plague, wherewith the LORD will smite the heathen that come not up to keep the feast of tabernacles." (Zechariah 14:17-18)

Prophecy No. 129
A Coup Will Take Place Against Christ's Rule
"And when the thousand years are expired, Satan shall be loosed out of his prison, And shall go out to deceive the nations which are in the four quarters of the earth, Gog, and Magog [old European name for Russia], to gather them together to battle: the number of whom is as the sand of the sea. And they went up on the breadth of the earth, and compassed the camp of the saints about, and the beloved city [Jerusalem]: and fire came down from God out of heaven, and devoured them." (Revelation 20:7-9)

Prophecy No. 130
The Deceiver to be Cast Into the Lake of Fire

"And the devil that deceived them was cast into the lake of fire and brimstone, where the beast and the false prophet are, and shall be tormented day and night for ever and ever." (Revelation 20:10)

Prophecy No. 131
Christ Holds Court

"For the Father judgeth no man, but hath committed all judgment unto the Son: That all men should honor the Son, even as they honor the Father. He that honoureth not the Son honoureth not the Father which hath sent him. Verily, verily, I say unto you, He that heareth my word, and believeth on him that sent me, hath everlasting life, and shall not come into condemnation...Verily, verily, I say unto you, The hour is coming, and now is, when the dead shall hear the voice of the Son of God: and they that hear shall live. For as the Father hath life in himself; so hath he given to the Son to have life in himself; And hath given him authority to execute judgment also, because he is the Son of man. Marvel not at this: for the hour is coming, in the which all that are in the graves shall hear his voice, And shall come forth; they that have done good, unto the resurrection of life; and they that have done evil, unto the resurrection of damnation... And the Father himself, which hath sent me, hath borne witness of me... And ye have not his word abiding in you: for whom he hath sent, him ye believe not. Search the scriptures; for in them ye think ye have eternal life: and they are they which testify of me. And ye will not come to me, that ye might have life." (Jesus Christ, the Son of God – John 5:22-40)

✓ Hear O Israel the LORD our God is one LORD. (Deut. 6:4)

✓ "Every knee shall bow to me and every tongue confess to God …. that Jesus Christ is Lord to the glory of God the father." (Rom 14:11; Philp 2:11)

✓ "For we must all appear before the judgment seat of Christ; that every one may receive the things *done* in *his* body, according to that he hath done, whether *it be* good or bad." (2 Cor 5:10)

✓ Jesus Christ, the Son of God, stated, "I and my father are one." (John 10:30)

✓ "If you have seen me you have seen the father." (John 10:30)

✓ "Do not think that I will accuse you to the Father: there is one that accuseth you, even Moses, in whom ye trust. For had ye believed Moses, ye would have believed me: for he wrote of me." (John 5:45-46.)

✓ The last book of the Bible by its full title is called "The Revelation of Jesus Christ" revealing that He and the Father are one. The same one who stated, "Let Us [plural] make man in Our [plural] on image [singular]. "Hear O Israel the LORD thy God is one LORD." The revealed "one Lord" is the revelation of Lord Jesus Christ being Emmanuel interpreted as God with us. (See: Did the God of Israel have a Son? What did the Jewish Prophets Say?)

Prophecy No. 132
The Great White Throne Judgment Day

"And I saw a great white throne, and him that sat on it, from whose face the earth and the heaven fled away; and there was found no place for them. And I saw the dead, small and great, stand before God; and the books were opened: and another book was opened, which is the book of life: and the dead were judged out of those things which were written in the books, according to their works. And the sea gave up the dead which were in it; and death and hell delivered up the dead which were in them: and they were judged every man according to their works. And death and hell were cast into the lake of fire. This is the second death. And whosoever was not found written in the book of life was cast into the lake of fire." (Revelation 20:11-15)

✓ "… he shall be tormented with fire and brimstone in the presence of the holy angels, and in the presence of the Lamb: And the smoke of their torment ascendeth up for ever and ever: and they have no rest day nor night…" (Revelation 14:10-11)

✓ "Because they rebelled against the words of God, and contemned the counsel of the most High: Therefore he brought down their heart with labor; they fell down, and there was none to help." (Psalms 107:11-12)

✓ "Behold, is it not of the LORD of hosts that the people shall <u>labor in the very fire</u>, and the people shall weary themselves for very vanity?" (The Prophet Habakkuk 2:13)

✓ "The wicked shall be turned into hell, and all the nations that forget God." (Psalm 9:17)

✓ Ministers who thought that placing faith in Christ was too easy to obtain the gift of eternal life, but rather used their good works to make Jesus their "Lord" will be cast into hell because eternal life is a gift by faith and not by works. Jesus Christ stated, "Many will say to me in that day, Lord, Lord, have we not prophesied [preached] in thy name? And in thy name have cast out devils? And in thy name done many wonderful works? And then will I profess unto them, I never knew you: depart from me, ye that work iniquity." (Matt. 7:22-23) Salvation is a free gift by having faith in Jesus, and not by doing good works for it. "For by the works of the law shall no flesh living be justified." (Acts 16:31, Rom. 3:20) Jesus informed His Jewish brethren, "Do not think that I will accuse you to the Father: there is one that accuseth you, even Moses, in whom ye trust. For had ye believed Moses, ye would have believed me; for he wrote of me. But if ye believe not his writings, how shall ye believe my words?" (John 5:45-47)

✓ "Believe on the Lord Jesus Christ and thou shalt be saved." (Acts 16:31) For the only unforgivable sin is not receiving forgiveness of sin coupled with life eternal by believing in Christ Jesus. Read our free book online <u>One Hundred Reasons Why Born Again Believers Cannot Lose their Salvation</u>: *Salvation by Grace Explained. Available free* at www.HaveYouHeardTheGoodNews.com.

Prophecy No. 133
Jesus Abdicates Israel's Throne to David As King

"And I will set up one shepherd over them and he shall feed them even my servant David; he shall feed them, and he shall be their shepherd. And I the LORD will be their God, and my servant David a prince among them; I the LORD have spoken it. And I will make with them a covenant of peace, and will cause the evil beasts to cease out of the land: and they shall dwell safely in the wilderness, and sleep in the woods. And I will make them and the places round about my hill a blessing; and I will cause the shower to come down in his season; there shall be showers of blessing. And the tree of the field shall yield her fruit, and the earth shall yield her increase, and they shall be safe in their land, and shall know that I am the LORD, when I have broken the bands of their yoke, and delivered them out of the hand of those that served themselves of them. And they shall no more be a prey to the heathen, neither shall the beast of the land devour them; but they shall dwell safely, and none shall make them afraid. And I will raise up for them a plant of renown, and they shall be no more consumed with hunger in the land, neither bear the shame of the heathen any more. Thus shall they know that I the LORD their God am with them, and that they, even the house of Israel, are my people, saith the Lord GOD. And ye my flock, the flock of my pasture, are men, and I am your God, saith the Lord GOD... They will live in the land I gave to my servant Jacob, the land where your fathers lived. They and their children and their children's children will live there forever, and David my servant will be their prince forever..." (Ezekiel 34:23-31, 37:25)

Prophecy No. 134
The Day of the Lord Followed by the Day of God

"But the **day of the Lord** [Christ's reign of a thousand years] will come as a thief in the night; in the which the heavens shall pass away with a great noise, and the elements [earth, water, fire, air] shall melt with fervent heat, the earth also and the works that are therein shall be burned up. Seeing then that all these things shall be dissolved, what manner of persons ought ye to be in all holy conversation [lifestyle] and godliness, Looking for and hasting unto the coming of the **day of God** [the rulership of God throughout eternity], wherein the heavens being on fire shall be dissolved, and the elements shall melt with fervent heat? Nevertheless we, according to his promise, look for new heavens and a new earth, wherein dwelleth righteousness." (2 Peter 3:10-13)

Prophecy No. 135
Lifespan of Earth Inhabitants Increased

"And I saw a new heaven and a new earth: for the first heaven and the first earth were passed away; and there was no more sea." (Revelation 21:1) "□For, behold, I create new heavens and a new earth: and the former shall not be remembered, nor come into mind. But be ye glad and rejoice forever in that which I create: for, behold, I create Jerusalem a rejoicing, and her people a joy. And I will rejoice in Jerusalem, and joy in my people: and the voice of weeping shall be no more heard in her, nor the voice of crying. There shall be no more thence an infant of days, nor an old man that hath not filled his days: for the child shall die an hundred years old; but the sinner being an hundred years old shall be accursed." (Isaiah 65:17-20)

✓ Under His reign of righteousness, one can live up to 100 years and then must submit to Christ as Lord or be accursed (put to death). Capital punishment will be on earth when Christ rules with "a rod of iron."

✓ Death will exist for a time in new heaven & new earth.

Prophecy No. 136
Christ Restores Heaven & Earth Back to His Father As Perfect the Last Enemy, Death is Destroyed

"Then cometh the end, when he shall have delivered up the kingdom to God, even the Father; when he shall have put down all rule and all authority and power. For he must reign, till he hath put all enemies under his feet. The last enemy that shall be destroyed is death....And when all things shall be subdued unto him, then shall the Son also himself be subject unto him that put all things under him, that God may be all in all." (1 Corinthians 15: 24-28)

Prophecy No. 137
Christ Reigns as King of Kings From New Jerusalem

"And I saw a new heaven and a new earth: for the first heaven and the first earth were passed away; and there was no more sea. And I John saw the holy city, new Jerusalem, coming down from God out of heaven, prepared as a bride adorned for her husband. And I heard a great voice out of heaven saying, Behold, the tabernacle of God is with men, and he will dwell with them, and they shall be his people, and God himself shall be with them, and be their God. And God shall wipe away all tears from their eyes; and there shall be no more death, neither sorrow, nor crying, neither shall there be any more pain: for the former things are passed away. And he that sat upon the throne said, Behold, I make all things new. And he said unto me, Write: for these words are true and faithful." (Revelation 21:1-5)

Prophecy No. 138
God's Plan for Ages to Come

"That <u>in the ages to come</u> he might show the exceeding riches of his grace in his kindness toward us through Christ Jesus.... To the intent that now unto the principalities and powers in heavenly places might be known by the church [the redeemed] the manifold wisdom of God."   (Eph. 2:7, 3:10)

Section Ten: Signs of His Second Coming

Prophecy No. 139
A Party Atmosphere Prevails Prior to Lord's Return
"Heaven and earth shall pass away but my words shall not pass away. And take heed to yourselves, lest at any time your hearts be overcharged with surfeiting [partying], and drunkenness, and cares of this life, and so that day come upon you unawares. For as a snare shall it come on all them that dwell on the face of the whole earth. Watch ye therefore, and pray always, that ye may be accounted worthy to escape all these things that shall come to pass, and to stand before the Son of man." (Luke 21:33-36)

Prophecy No. 140
Church Leaders Departing From the Faith
"Now the Spirit speaketh expressly, that in the latter times some shall depart from the faith, giving heed to seducing spirits, and doctrines of devils." (1 Timothy. 4:1)

✓ Church leadership involvement in ministry scandals

✓ Child molestation charges against church ministers

✓ Church leaders departing from the faith to teach universal salvation
✓ Church leadership ordaining gays against church doctrine
✓ Church leadership in sex scandals

✓ Church leadership performing gay marriages

✓ Bibles, such as the New International Version (NIV) remove Satan's name "Lucifer" and insert Christ's title of "morning star" in its place without church protest. (Isa. 14:12, NIV)

✓ The only way books can be copyrighted is to be "significantly different" from the original manuscript and copyrighted Bibles are no different. Therefore, many new Bibles have *subtly* changed the doctrine that salvation is by grace through faith alone in Christ alone, to make salvation by virtuous works plus God's grace, and modern theologians changed the word in Bibles from patience to *perseverance* which is a significantly different whereby they slyly introduce a lighter form of a works based salvation doctrine. (Romans 4:5)

Prophecy No. 141
Widespread Backsliding to be Common in the Church

"Let no man deceive you by any means: for that day shall not come, except there come a falling away first [Christians backsliding] ...." (2 Thessalonians 2:3)

Prophecy No. 142
Many Will Claim to be Christ

"For many shall come in my name, saying, I am Christ; and shall deceive many." (Matthew 24:5)

"Jesus answering said, Take heed lest any man deceive you: For **many shall come** in my name, **saying, I am Christ**; and shall deceive many. And when ye shall hear of wars and rumours of wars, be ye not troubled: such things must needs be; but the end shall not be yet." Jesus Christ - Mark 13:5-7

Some who claim to be Christ

Rev. Sun Myung Moon - Korea - Moonies

Rev. Jim Jones - Peoples' Temple Church

Jose Luis deJesus Miranda - S. America

David Koresh - Branch Davidians

Hale-Bop Comet - Marshall Applewhite

Charles Manson & "Many" More to Come

"…Take heed that ye be not deceived: for many shall come in my name, saying, I am Christ; and the time draweth near: go ye not therefore after them." (Luke 21:8)

Prophecy No. 143
Perfect Convergence of All Signs Manifest in One Generation

"So likewise ye, when ye shall see all these things, know that it is near, even at the doors. Verily I say unto you, This generation shall not pass till all these things be fulfilled." (Matthew 24:33-34)

Prophecy No. 144
Perilous Times Shall Come

"This know also, that in the last days perilous times shall come. For men shall be lovers of their own selves, covetous, boasters, proud, blasphemers, disobedient to parents, unthankful, unholy, Without natural affection, trucebreakers, false accusers, incontinent, fierce, despisers of those that are good, Traitors, heady, high-minded, lovers of pleasures more than lovers of God; Having a form of godliness, but denying the power thereof: from such turn away. For of this sort are they which creep into houses, and lead captive silly women laden with sins, led away with divers lusts, Ever learning, and never able to come to the knowledge of the truth. Now as Jannes and Jambres withstood Moses, so do these also resist the truth: men of corrupt minds, reprobate concerning the faith. But they shall proceed no further: for their folly shall be manifest unto all men, as theirs also was." (Timothy 3:1-9)

✓ "For the wrath of God is revealed from heaven against all ungodliness and unrighteousness of men, who hold the truth in unrighteousness; Because that which may be known of God is manifest in them; for God hath shewed it unto them…. So that they are without excuse: Because that, when they knew God, they glorified him not as God, neither were thankful; but became vain in their imaginations, and their foolish heart was darkened. Professing themselves to be wise, they became fools, And changed the glory of the incorruptible God into an image made like to corruptible man, and to birds, and four-footed beasts, and creeping things. Wherefore God also gave them up to uncleanness through the lusts of their own hearts, to dishonor their own bodies between themselves: Who changed the truth of God into a lie, and worshipped and served the creature more than the Creator, who is blessed for ever. Amen. For this cause God gave them up unto vile affections: for even their women did change the natural use into that which is against nature: And likewise also the men, leaving the natural use of the woman, burned in their lust one toward another; men with men working that which is unseemly, and receiving in themselves that recompense of their error which was meet. And even as they did not like to retain God in their knowledge, God gave them over to a reprobate mind, to do those things which are not convenient; ☐Being filled with all unrighteousness, fornication, wickedness, covetousness, maliciousness; full of envy, murder, debate, deceit, malignity; whisperers, Backbiters, haters of God, despiteful, proud, boasters, inventors of evil things, disobedient to parents, ☐Without understanding, covenant breakers, without natural affection, implacable, unmerciful: Who knowing the judgment of God, that they which commit such things are worthy of death, not only do the same, but have pleasure in them that do them." (Romans 1:18-32)

✓ Scoffers and skeptics will begin mocking Christians who will begin proclaiming seven years, prematurely that Jesus is coming soon. Peter prophesied that many will say, "Where is the promise of his coming? For since the fathers fell asleep, all things continue as they were…" (2 Peter 3:4)

✓ According to Scripture, Jerusalem is the time-piece of the world, so "Pray for the peace of Jerusalem: they shall prosper that love thee." (Psalm 122:6)

✓ The opinion of the religious world will be "My Lord delayeth his coming…" (Matthew 24:48)

✓ While world opinion be, "The LORD will not do good, neither will he do evil." (The Prophet Zephaniah 1:12)

✓ At a time ye think not your Lord doth come. "What I say unto you I say unto you all. Watch!" (Mark 13:37)

Prophecy No. 145
No Man Knows The Day or Hour of Christ's Return

"…when ye shall see these things come to pass, know that it is nigh, even at the doors. Verily I say unto you, that this generation shall not pass, till all these things be done. Heaven and earth shall pass away: but my words shall not pass away. But of that day and that hour knoweth no man, no, not the angels which are in heaven, neither the Son, but the Father. Take ye heed, watch and pray: for ye know not when the time is." (Mark 13:29-33)

Prophecy No. 146
Signs of the Times

"O ye hypocrites, ye can discern the face of the sky; but can ye not discern the signs of the times?" (Matthew 16:3)

"And when these things begin to come to pass, then look up, and lift up your heads; for your redemption draweth nigh. ...So likewise ye, when ye see these things come to pass, know ye that the kingdom of God is nigh at hand. ... And take heed to yourselves, ... and so that day come upon you unawares. For as a snare shall it come on all them that dwell on the face of the whole earth." (Luke 21:28-35)

Prophecy No. 147
Crime Increase to Cause Love of Many to Wax Cold

"And many false prophets shall rise, and shall deceive many. And because iniquity shall abound, the love of many shall wax cold. But as the days of Noah were [when violence covered the earth], so shall also the coming of the Son of man be. For as in the days that were before the flood they were eating and drinking, marrying and giving in marriage, until the day that Noe entered into the ark, And knew not until the flood came, and took them all away; so shall also the coming of the Son of man be." (Matthew 24:11-12, 37-39)

Luke 21:26 / Genesis 6:13
"As violence covered the earth as in the days of Noah, so shall it be at the coming of the son of man [Christ]."

School Shootings	Mall Shootings
Movie Shooting	Car bombings
Boston Bombing	Pakistan Bombing
Terrorism in Britain	Terrorism in Spain
Bombing in Nigeria	Violence in Sudan
Afghan War	Iraqi War
Muslims murdering Non-Muslims in Africa	
Bombings in France	Yemen bombings
Mob violence in game	9/11 Terrorist Attacks
Bombing in Turkey	Bombing in Lebanon
Suicide bombing In Iraq	Suicide bombing in Israel
Family Violence	Bullying and Hate Crimes
Drone Strikes	Government Assassinations

"As it was in the days of Noah so shall it be at the coming of the son of Man." According to the Genesis account of Noah's lifetime, God intended to destroy mankind's existence "for the earth was filled with violence through them. Therefore, I will destroy them with the earth. But Noah found grace in the eyes of the LORD." (Genesis 6: 13)

Violent shootings increased in the United States; 3,200 people shot in Chicago (2016), 14 at a San Bernardino office party, 4 at a Killen, TX military base, 26 at Sandy Hook's elementary school, 32 at Virginia Tech, 50 at an Orlando club, and 5 Dallas police by a sniper. *This sadly, added on October 1, 2017. The deadliest shooting in recent history at a country music show in Las Vegas, Nevada killing 59 people with 527 injured.*

✓ Unfortunately, these "are the beginning of sorrows" according to Jesus (Matt. 24:8) There will be more violence to come. In "the days of Noah" violence filled the earth, "so shall it be in the days the son of man." (Gen. 6:13; Luke 17:26) "Even so, Come Lord Jesus." (Rev. 22:20)

Prophecy No. 148
He Will Return Quickly
"He was in the world and the world was made by him, and the world knew him not... □He which testifieth these things saith, Surely I come quickly. Amen. Even so, come, Lord Jesus. The grace of our Lord Jesus Christ be with you all. Amen." (John 1:10, Revelation 22:20-21)

Watch!
"At a time ye think not your Lord doth come. What I say unto you I say unto you all. Watch." (Jesus Christ: Mark 13:37)

Prophecy No. 149
How To Escape the Wrath to Come

"Believe on Jesus the Messiah and you shall be saved"

Romans 10:9-10 states that if you confess with your mouth that Jesus is Lord and Believe in you heart that God raised him from the dead, you shall be saved. For with the mouth confession is made for salvation and with the heart man believeth unto righteousness.

Acts 16:31 "Believe on the Lord Jesus Christ and thou shalt be saved."

Our faith is counted for righteousness not our good works Romans 4:5 "To him that works not but believes on Him that justifies the ungodly, his faith is counted for righteousness. "without faith it is impossible to please God" and "the law is not of faith" the "law was our school-master to bring us to Christ (Messiah) that we might be justifed by faith." He that has the Son has life eternal.

Jesus Christ indicated the nearness of the rapture when he stated, **"When these things begin to come to pass, then look up, for your redemption draweth nigh."** (Luke 21:28) You need a savior, the same one who warned you of all this. **NO OTHER RELIGION CAN NOR TRIES TO INFORM YOU OF THE FUTURE WITH THIS TYPE OF ACCURACY.** Only the Lord God can do this, and He had it written down thousands of years before He sent His only Son, Jesus Christ, into the world to save those who believe in Him. Since "confession is made unto salvation," to escape the wrath that is to come, you must "…confess with your mouth that Jesus is Lord, and believe in your heart that God raised Him from the dead, and thou shall be saved." (Romans 10:9-10) By repenting of your sin of unbelief in Christ as Savior, your faith in Christ is counted for righteousness, not your good deeds, great behavior, moral excellence, or keeping the commandments. If you try to stand before God by your integrity, morality, or character in other words your self-righteousness, then you make God a fool for having sent His Son to die for your sins for evidently you didn't need it. Your good works can never save you. Only belief in the death and resurrection of God's own Son does that "For God so loved the world that He gave his only Son that whosoever believes in him should not perish but have everlasting life." (John 3:16) If you refuse to believe this simple message, please keep this Prophecy Checklist handy. You will certainly need it during the Great Tribulation that is coming upon the earth. "But he that believeth not is condemned…" (John 3:18) "Believe on the Lord Jesus Christ (works of his death, blood, and resurrection for you) and thou shalt be saved…" (Acts 16:31)

"It pleased God by the foolishness of preaching to save them that believe. For the preaching of the cross is to them that perish foolishness; but unto us which are saved it is the power of God." (1 Corinthians 1:21, 18) For salvation [eternal life] is to "him that worketh not (at being good enough to be saved), but believeth in him that justifieth the <u>ungodly</u> [that's you and I], his faith is counted for righteousness." (Romans 4:5) Salvation is for sinners! What must I do to get the Second Birth? "Ask and you shall receive." Simply pray, "I believe Jesus is Lord and God raised him from the dead. Come into my heart, Lord Jesus. I want to be saved. Amen." At this moment, you have experienced the new birth with the divine nature of Jesus Christ being born into your heart as your Savior as well as your sinless life before God. You now have been granted "eternal salvation, eternal redemption, and eternal life" according to God's promise. Although you cannot feel Him, touch Him, see Him or taste Him, you now have Christ's divine nature in you (your ticket to heaven) that cannot sin and will never leave or forsake you. However, you also still have the nature of sin, human nature, laced with its sinful habits. Your outward lifestyle has not been transformed. Transformation of lifestyle will be the result of your purposeful pursuit of spiritual growth in grace. (Titus 2:11-13) By praying this prayer in faith, you only received the gift of salvation which is the "free gift" of eternal life. You have not become a disciple of Jesus Christ until you commit to studying the Apostle Paul's and the other Apostles' "instructions in righteousness." To become Christ's disciple you must deny yourself, but to become saved takes only an act of your faith in what Christ has done for you in dying for your sins and rising

again to pay for your gift of eternal life, eternal salvation, and eternal redemption. *"For God sent not his Son into the world to condemn the world; but that the world through him might be saved. He that believeth on him is not condemned; but he that believeth not is condemned already, because he hath not believeth in the name of the only begotten Son of God."* (John 3:16) "Whosoever calleth upon the name of the Lord shall be saved...for there is none other name under heaven given among men whereby we must be saved." (Acts 2:21, 4:12) Therefore, "Believe on the Lord Jesus Christ and thou shalt be saved." (Acts 16:31)

For more information on the permanence of your eternal salvation *a free book* is available *online* titled <u>One Hundred Reasons Why Born Again Believers Cannot Lose Their Salvation</u>. You may read it free. Its available at HaveYouHeardTheGoodNews.com

Prophecy No. 150
The Rapture of the Church Will Take Place Before This Great Tribulation Strikes Earth

"I also will keep thee from the hour of temptation [tribulation], which shall come upon all the world, to try them that dwell upon the earth." (Jesus Christ: Revelation 3:10)

"For God hath not appointed us to wrath [the Great Tribulation], but to obtain salvation by our Lord Jesus Christ." (1 Thessalonians 5:9)

"...ye turned to God from idols to serve the living and true God; And to wait for his Son from heaven, whom he raised from the dead, even Jesus, which delivered us from the wrath to come [the time of Jacob's (Israel's) trouble]." (1 Thessalonians 1:9-10)

"The blessed hope" that theologians call *the rapture* of the Church was prophesied by the Apostle Paul who wrote, "I would not have you to be ignorant, brethren, concerning them which are asleep, [dead] that ye sorrow not, even as others which have no hope. For if we believe that Jesus died and rose again, even so them also which sleep [died] in Jesus will God bring with him. For this we say unto you by the word of the Lord, that we which are alive and remain unto the coming of the Lord shall not prevent [precede] them which are asleep [dead]. For the Lord himself shall descend from heaven with a shout, with the voice of the archangel, and with the trump [trumpet] of God: and the dead in Christ shall rise first: Then we which are alive and remain shall be caught up together with them in the clouds, to meet the Lord in the air: and so shall we ever be with the Lord. Wherefore, comfort one another with these words." (1 Thessalonians 4:13-18)

"Behold, I shew you a mystery; We shall not all sleep [die], but we shall all be changed, In a moment, in the twinkling of an eye, at the last trump: for the trumpet shall sound, and the dead shall be raised incorruptible, and we shall be changed. For this corruptible must put on incorruption, and this mortal must put on immortality." (1 Corinthians 15:51-53)

Prophecy No. 151
After the Rapture All Believers Must Appear Before the Judgment Seat of Christ

"For we must all appear before the judgment seat of Christ; that every one may receive the things done in his body, according to that he hath done, whether it be good or bad. Every man's work shall be made manifest: for the day shall declare it, because it shall be revealed by fire; and the fire shall try every man's work of what sort it is. If any man's work abide which he hath built thereupon, he shall receive a reward. If any man's work shall be burned, he shall suffer loss: but he himself shall be saved; yet so as by fire." (2 Corinthians 5:10, 1 Corinthians 3:13-15)

✓ The believer's lifetime sins have already been washed away by the blood of Christ. Only the works of the believers will be judged.

Prophecy No. 152
The Marriage Supper

"Let us be glad and rejoice, and give honor to him: for the marriage of the Lamb is come, and his wife [the church of believers in Christ] hath made herself ready. ☐☐And to her was granted that she should be arrayed in fine linen clean and white:... the righteousness of saints. ☐And he saith unto me, Write, Blessed are they which are called unto the marriage supper of the Lamb. And he saith unto me, These are the true sayings of God." (Revelation 19:7-9)

Prophecy No. 153
Bridal Feast

"And I say unto you, That many shall come from the east and west, and shall sit down with Abraham, and Isaac, and Jacob, in the kingdom of heaven." (Matthew 8:11)

Prophecy No. 154
Christ Will Receive Those He Redeemed To Himself

"In my Father's house are many mansions: if it were not so, I would have told _you_. I go to prepare a place for _you_. And if I go and prepare a place for _you_, I will come again [His Second Coming], and receive _you_ unto myself; that where I am, there _ye_ may be also...I am the way, the truth, and the life: no man cometh unto the Father, but by me."
(John 14:2, 3, 6)

Prophecy No. 155
The Last Words of Jesus Christ in the Book of The Revelation

"He which testifieth these things saith, Surely I come quickly. Amen. Even so, come, Lord Jesus." (Revelation 22:20)

"But, beloved, be not ignorant of this one thing, that one day is with the Lord as a thousand years, and a thousand years as one day." (2 Peter 3:8)

In light of this, according to Christ's timetable it has only been _two days_ to Him (but 2,000 years to us) since His crucifixion and resurrection. Therefore, to him, He is returning quickly for its only been two days since His first appearance.

✓ All these prophecies were predicted by Jewish men who foretold of a coming Jewish Messiah who, like Joseph of the Old Testament would be rejected by his brethren, and, like Joseph, His name would become great among the Gentiles according to the Prophet Malachi. (Malachi 1:11) This is none other than the name of Jesus Christ, whom the Old Testament prophet Micah foretold would be born in Bethlehem. (Micah 5:2)

Prophecy No. 156
The Time Is At Hand...
"This is the revelation of Jesus Christ, which God gave to him, to show unto his servants things which must shortly come to pass.... Blessed is he that readeth, and they that hear the words of this prophecy, and keep those things which are written therein: for the time is at hand." (Revelation 1:1, 3)

"Heaven and earth shall pass away, but my words shall never pass away". Jesus Christ

"Lord, who hath believed our Report?" Isaiah 53:1

"Believe On The Lord Jesus Christ and thou shall be saved and thy household." (Acts 16:31)

Jesus said, "For God so loved the world that he gave his own begotten son that whosoever believes in him shall not perish but have everlasting life. For God sent not his son into the world to condemn the world but that the world may be saved through him. He that believes is not condemned, but he who believes not is condemned already because he has not believed in the authority of the only begotten son." (John 3:16-19)

Section Eleven: The Biblical History of Iraq

The history of Iraq is found in the book of beginnings known as Genesis in Scripture. Elementary schools oftentimes teach Iraq's history in early civilization when it was called Mesopotamia which means "land between two rivers." This historic land has two of the oldest rivers known to man flowing through its borders, the Tigris and Euphrates rivers. (Genesis 2:14) These same rivers flowed through the garden of Eden when Iraq was known as Assyria (Asshuria) founded by Asshur a Semite/Shemite, according to the King James Version of the Bible. (Gen. 10:11) The land we know today as Iraq had additional names. It has been called various names throughout history such as Persia, Babylon, Media of the Medes, and Ur of the Chaldees.

UR = BABYLON = PERSIA=ASSYRIA=MEDIA

Iraq is the birthplace of the most famous man in the world, although western civilization and the Far East are almost totally ignorant of his importance to world history. The man's name was Abraham, the friend of God, and three major religions of the world trace their roots back to him. When Abraham was born in the district we call Iraq today but was called "Ur of the Chaldees" in his time. (Gen. 11:28) According to Boyd's Bible Dictionary, the word *Ur* means region and the word *Chaldees* means demons. Hence, Abram, who later was renamed Abraham by God, was born in what is known as a "region of demons."

It is interesting that this mysterious place we know as Iraq was known in ancient times as Ur of the Chaldees i.e., a region of demons. God told Abram to remove himself from that land and go to a land that He would show him and Abram obeyed. When the Jewish descendants of Abraham were brought into this land as slaves, a young Jewish boy named Daniel was brought before the king of this region renamed Babylon. When Daniel was older, he went without food for twenty-one days in prayer to the God of the Israelites. (Dan. 10:3) On the twenty-first day, an angel appeared unto Daniel and informed him that he had to fight the demon principality assigned over this district called Persia, and it took him twenty-one days to fight with the assistance of Michael the Archangel to get Daniel the answer to his prayer. Daniel wrote that an angel appeared to him and stated: "Fear not, Daniel: for from the first day that thou didst set thine heart to understand, and to chasten thyself before thy God, thy words were heard, and I am come for thy words. But **the prince of the kingdom of Persia withstood me one and twenty days**: but, lo, **Michael, one of the chief princes, came to help me;** and I remained there with the kings of Persia. Now I am come to make thee understand <u>what shall befall thy people [Jews] in the latter days</u>: for yet the vision is for many days." (Daniel 10:12-14)

A demonic principality, known as the *Prince of Persia* was resisting the angelic messenger that was sent from God with the answer to Daniel's prayer the first day he prayed. Ur of the Chaldees, then renamed the Kingdom of Persia, had an assigned demon to that region of demons to withstand God's messenger and message.

Iraq and the Bottom of the River Euphrates

Ironically, according to the Revelation of Jesus Christ, the last book in the Bible, God has chained four fallen angels (demons) in the bottom of the Euphrates River that flows through Iraq, and these fallen angels, i.e. demons, shall be released in the end times to slay one third of mankind on the face of the earth.

"And the sixth angel sounded, and I heard a voice from the four horns of the golden altar which is before God, Saying to the sixth angel which had the trumpet, **Loose the four angels which are bound in the great river Euphrates. And the four angels were loosed, which were prepared for an hour, and a day, and a month, and a year, for to slay the third part of men**." (Revelation 9:13-15)

Iraq, formerly called Ur of the Chaldees interpreted a *region of demons*, has at this present hour four fallen angels, i.e. demons, bound in the bottom of the Great River Euphrates "in chains under the darkness" for a preset day, month, year, and hour to be loosed to execute the judgment of the wrath of God to slay one third of unrepentant mankind from the face of the earth. (Jude 15) *Believe it or not!*

Section Twelve: God's Holy Day Timetable

The Prophetic Fulfillment Of Jewish Holidays Declare God's Timetable

The Old Testament foreshadows or foretells events to be fulfilled in the New Testament. In the Old Testament, God commanded Israel to observe seven holy days, called holidays by gentiles in modern times. Through the exact observance of these specific Jewish holy days, God fulfilled Bible prophecy thousands of years later on the exact day. In these end times, God will demonstrate the fulfillment of these Jewish holidays with the climax of the Second Coming. Watch.

The First Holy Day:The Feast of Passover – Initiated

This was the day that God commanded Moses to tell the Jews to observe forever. It is in celebration of the night that God commanded perfectly flawless lambs to be slain and the blood of the lambs to be placed on the doorpost of all the homes of Jewish slaves in North Africa (Egypt). God sent his death angel throughout the land of Egypt. When it saw the blood of the lamb on the doorpost, all parties in that home were given immunity from the death angel's grasp that night and freed from slavery the next morning. Those who refused to apply the lamb's blood to the doorpost of their dwelling had the firstborn of the household slain that fateful night.

The Feast of Passover – Fulfilled

Two thousand years later, "the lamb of God that taketh away the sin of the world" appeared in the person of Jesus Christ. On the exact day of the Jewish feast of Passover, Jesus Christ, as the "lamb of God," was hung on a cross, crucified for the sins of the world that all who believe in their heart that His death, blood, and resurrection was payment enough for their lifetime sin-debt would be spared the second death, called eternal damnation and given eternal life. The Jewish Apostle Paul wrote that Christ, the King of the Jews, is our Passover lamb. (1 Corinthians 5:7) Christ died for the sins of the world on the same day as the observance of the Feast of Passover. (John 19:14) Our firstborn, human nature, is a slave of sin but when the "Son sets you free you shall be free indeed," by His divine nature born again in you, once His blood is applied to the doorpost of your heart.

The Second Holy Day:
The Feast of Unleavened Bread – Initiated

On the night that Jews were to eat the Passover Lamb, they were also to partake of the bread that had no leaven (yeast) in it - *unleavened bread.* They were commanded not to put yeast in their bread that night because they would not have time for it to *rise* before Pharaoh would drive them out of the land of Egypt. Jews, on this holiday, take the middle piece of bread and break it. The bread is flat as a wafer, and has many stripes and is pierced. Jews call it matzoth.

The Feast of Unleavened Bread – Fulfilled

Two thousand years later, Jesus Christ was born in Bethlehem, a name that means house of bread. Later He began calling Himself the Bread of Life that came down from heaven.(John 6:31-36) Anyone who partakes of Him will have everlasting life. Leaven or yeast to the Jews is symbolic of sin's corruption. On the exact observance of this holiday, Jesus Christ, the bread of life, took the middle piece of bread and broke it uttering the fulfillment of this holiday's symbol saying, "This is my body which is broken for you." Christ's sinless broken body hung on the middle cross as our sin offering "wounded for our transgressions and bruised for our iniquities…with … stripes…" (Isa. 53:5) As the Jews' matzoth bread has stripes all over it and is pierced, so the body of Christ was whipped with many stripes and pierced in his crucifixion for mankind. While in the tomb, as foretold by the Jew's King David, Christ's body did not see corruption [decay]. (Psalms 16:10) On the exact observance of this holiday, the body of Christ was lying sinless in the tomb, covered with stripes and pierced like unleavened bread. As leaven or yeast, which typifies sin, was not added to this type of bread, Christ, sinless body, the bread of life had not yet *risen* from the dead.

The Third Holy Day:
The Feast of Firstfruits – Initiated

God said to Moses, "Speak unto the children of Israel, and say unto them, When ye be come into the land which I give unto you, and shall reap the harvest thereof, then ye shall bring a sheaf of the firstfruits of your harvest unto the priest: And he shall wave the sheaf before the LORD, to be accepted for you: on the morrow after the Sabbath the priest shall wave it." (Leviticus 23:10-11)

Feast of Firstfruits – Fulfilled

The third day in Scripture is always typical of resurrection, whether it was the third day of creation and the dry land appeared, or Jonah emerging from the belly of the whale on the third day, and this third Jewish holy day is no different. On the exact day of the observance of this Jewish Feast of Firstfruits, Jesus Christ rose from the dead, and became "the firstfruits of them that slept [had died]." (1st Corinthians 15:20) Jesus Christ was raised from the dead on observance of the day of the Feast of Firstfruits, the morning *after* the Sabbath (Saturday).

The Fourth Holy Day:
The Feast of Pentecost – Initiated

This feast was declared to observe the day that the Ten Commandments of Moses' Law were given to the Jews at Mount Sinai and 3,000 people died.

The Feast of Pentecost – Fulfilled

Two thousand years later, on the exact observance of this feast called Pentecost, the church was born.

"When the day of Pentecost was fully come, they were all with one accord in one place. And suddenly there came a sound from heaven as of a rushing mighty wind, and it filled all the house where they were sitting.... And they were filled with the holy Ghost, and began to speak with other tongues, as the Spirit gave them utterance. And ... devout men thought they were drunk with new wine... and Peter spake saying, "Whosoever shall call on the name of the Lord shall be saved. Ye men of Israel, hear these words, Jesus of Nazareth, a man approved of God among you by miracles, which God did by him in the midst of you, as ye yourselves know. Him, have you taken with wicked hands and crucified and slain. Whom God has raised up, having loosed him from death: because it was impossible for him to be held by it even as David said.... Therefore let all the house of Israel know assuredly, that God has made the same Jesus, whom ye have crucified, both Lord and Christ. When they heard this they were pricked to their hearts, and asked, What must we do to be saved? Repent [of your unbelief and believe on Jesus Christ.] "Then they that gladly received his word were baptized and the same day 3,000 were added to the church." (Excerpts from Acts Chapter 2)

The Fifth Holy Day:
Feast of Trumpets – (Rosh Hashanah) Initiated:

This holiday is in observance of the Jewish New Year, Rosh Hashanah. In ancient times a Jewish priest would take a trumpet, called a Shofar, and blow it. At the sound of this primitive trumpet, the people would stop what they were doing and gather at the temple as one body of worshippers on this Feast of Trumpets. This feast is celebrated in the month of September or sometimes early October. Jews celebrate it as Rosh Hashanah.

The Feast of Trumpets Will Be Fulfilled

Though, "no man knows the day or the hour of the coming of the Lord," this is not the Coming of the Lord, but represents the blessed hope theologians call rapture of the church, which is to occur on the observance of the Feast of Trumpets.

"Behold, I shew you a mystery; We shall not all sleep, but we shall all be changed, In a moment, in the twinkling of an eye, at the last trump: for <u>the trumpet shall sound,</u> and the dead shall be raised incorruptible, and we shall be changed. For this corruptible must put on incorruption, and this mortal must put on immortality. So when this corruptible shall have put on incorruption, and this mortal shall have put on immortality, then shall be brought to pass the saying that is written, Death is swallowed up in victory." (1 Corinthians 15:51-54)

"For the Lord Himself shall descend from heaven with a shout, with the voice of the archangel, and <u>with the trump</u> <u>[trumpet] of God</u>: and the dead in Christ shall rise first: Then we which are alive and remain shall be caught up together with them in the clouds, to meet the Lord in the air: and so shall we ever be with the Lord." (1 Thessalonians 4:16-17)

In keeping with the timetable of these literally God-given Jewish holidays, the fulfillment of the Trumpet Feast known as Rosh Hashanah, that being the blessed hope known as the rapture, will occur in the month of September or possibly early October during the Feast of Trumpets, although the year is clearly unknown, the Apostle Paul lets us know that we are not to be ignorant of "the times and the seasons" of the day of the Lord. (1 Thessalonians 5:1)

The Sixth Holy Day:
The Day of Atonement – (Yom Kippur) Initiated:

This was the day when the high priest of Israel went into the holy of holies to sprinkle lamb's blood on the Ark of the Covenant (as seen in the Raiders of the Lost Ark) to obtain forgiveness for the nation of Israel's sins for a full year. The priest had bells and pomegranates on his garment that made sounds in the holy of holies, which indicated that God had not struck him dead for the sins of the people. The sound of these joy bells indicated that God accepted the lamb's blood as atonement for the sins of Israel and all Israel was saved from His wrath for a year. The Jews call this day Yom Kippur.

The Fulfillment of the Day of Atonement

This holiday generally occurs in the month of October. This is the only Israeli holiday in Scripture that is not called a feast. Its prophetic fulfillment will be the Second Coming of Jesus Christ, when "all Israel shall be saved" from annihilation from the armies of the world that will surround her on orders of the Anti-Semite/Antichrist, the global ruler from Persian region, today known as Iraq/Iran. (See Section Six: The Anti-Semite/Antichrist for more information). Although all of these God-designated Jewish holidays will be fulfilled on the exact day God established for their observance thousands of years ago, this particular day will not follow that established pattern because Jesus indicated that if it did no life would be spared alive on earth. Therefore, the days will be shortened so it can be fulfilled that no man will know the day or the hour of the coming of the Lord. (Matthew 25:13) Jesus said it this way, "Except those days should be shortened [by His coming], there should no flesh be saved; but for the elect's [Israel's] sake those days shall be shortened." (Matthew 24:22) (See Section Seven: The Coming of the Lord) On this day the Scripture will be literally fulfilled that "all Israel shall be saved," by the Lamb of God revealed from heaven, Jesus Christ. (Romans 11:26)

The Seventh Holy Day:
Feast of Tabernacles (Succoth/Sukkoth) Initiated

This is the last holy day that God commanded the Jews to observe. This holy day, as well as the other seven, is observed by Jews to this day. This holy day is known as the Feast of Booths in Leviticus chapter 23:33-43 where God commanded the Jews to build booths and stay in them seven days to commemorate how their forefathers lived after being freed from slavery in North Africa, Egypt called in Scripture "the land of Ham," named after Noah's second son. (Psalms 105:25,27, 106:22)

The Fulfillment of the Feast of Tabernacles

After the Second Coming of Christ, this feast will be spectacularly fulfilled when God Himself makes His tabernacle among men. Regarding Christ, the Greek Bibles states, "The Word was God and the Word was made flesh and *tabernacled* among us." (John 1:2) This feast will be fulfilled when "the tabernacle of God is with men, and he will dwell with them, and they shall be his people, and God himself shall be with them, and be their God." (Revelation. 21:3)   After Christ "thoroughly purges His floor," the floor in His Temple (called the Court of the Gentiles where Islam's Shrine of the Dome of the Rock sits), God will dwell in the same temple in Jerusalem where the Anti-Semite / Antichrist will have earlier declared himself God," and Jerusalem shall be the capital of the world and all nations shall flow up to it on the Feast of Tabernacles to honor God. Christ will decree that any nation that does not send delegates to Jerusalem on this holy day will have rain withheld from their land. (Zechariah. 14:17)

What must I do to be saved [receive eternal life and escape the wrath to come]? "…Believe on the Lord Jesus Christ, and thou shall be saved, and thy house. (Acts 16:31)

Does God Have A Son? Prophets say

According to the writings of the Jewish prophet Daniel, when three Hebrew men were cast into a burning fiery furnace for not bowing to Nebuchadnezzar, King of Babylon [Iraq], the Iraqi king looked into the fire and exclaimed, "Did we not cast three men bound into the fire? I see four men loose, walking in the midst of the fire, and they have no hurt; and the form of the fourth is like the Son of God." (Daniel 3:25) In Proverbs of King Solomon, the wisest of all men, also believed that the God of Israel, whom his father King David worshipped and served, had a Son. For Proverbs 30:4 states, "Who hath ascended up into heaven, or descended? Who hath gathered the wind in his fist? Who hath bound the waters in a garment? Who hath established all the ends of the earth? What is his name, and what is his son's name." (Proverbs 30:4) Therefore, God having a Son should not be a foreign concept to Jewish people for Isaiah, another Jewish prophet, foretold: "The Lord himself shall give you a sign; behold, a virgin shall conceive, and bear a son, and thou shall call his name Immanuel [interpreted, God with us]." (Isaiah 7:4) To date this sign has only been given to the Jewish race by way of The Virgin Miriam, Mary in English. The Jewish prophet also prophesied, "Unto us a child is born and unto us a son is given... and his name shall be called the mighty God, the Prince of Peace." (Isaiah 9:6) A son called "the mighty God"? The God of Israel declares that He is one, yet stated "Let Us make man in Our own image." The son born of the Jewish virgin declared, "I and my father are one." (John 10:30) Jesus Christ was the virgin born Son of God that was given to the nation of Israel as prophesied, and he fulfilled the prophecy of the Jewish Messiah that was to be born in Bethlehem per the Jewish prophet Micah. (Micah 5:2) Many Jewish people do not realize that Jesus Christ was Jewish and lived in a pro-Jewish way according to the laws of Moses. "For God so loved the world that He gave His only begotten Son that whosoever believeth in him should not perish but have everlasting life." (John 3:16) "In the beginning was the word and the word was with God and the word was God. He was in the world and the world was made by him and the world knew him not." (John 1:1,9) This God, known in Scripture as The God of Israel, had scribes and prophets of His chosen Hebrew people write that He declares the end from the beginning, and this prophecy checklist is where you can clearly see that He, the invisible God, alone is the true and the living God, and that His Son shall return according to His word.

The Prophecies we heard in church, we now see on television. Many people have ignored their Bibles to the point where prophecies are being fulfilled before their eyes and they don't recognize them. The Bible is the **_ONLY_** book that accurately foretells how things will end. No other religion's religious scriptures attempt this. Prophecy Checklist will keep you informed of the prophetic events that are unfolding as time ushers in the Second Coming of the Lord Jesus Christ!

"When you see these things begin to come to pass, look up for your redemption draweth nigh. Heaven and earth shall pass away but my words shall not pass away." Jesus the Christ/Messiah Lk 21:28, 33

If this book has been an eye opener for you, please do me a great favor by giving your feedback on it on Amazon.com. This may encourage those who do not attend church to obtain it and become informed for their salvation to believe on the Lord Jesus and be saved "for the time is at hand."

For a speaking engagement contact author by email at:

ministrymailnews@aol.com

"How is it you can predict the weather but cannot discern the signs of the times." - Jesus Christ (Matt 16:3) "As it was in the days of Noah (climate change flooding) so shall it be at the coming of the son of Man." - Jesus Christ (Luke 17:26) The sea and the waves roaring (hurricanes – Harvey, Irma, Katia, and Nate); - Jesus Christ (Lk 21:25)"As it was in the days of Lot (who lived in the legendary city of Sodom where Gay rights was the norm) so shall it be at the coming of the Son of Man." - Jesus Christ (Lk 17:28) "And ye shall hear of wars and rumors of wars (like the United States military being locked and loaded on North Korea) See that ye be not troubled: For all these things must come to pass, but the end is not yet." - Jesus Christ (Matt 24:6) For nation shall rise against nation, and kingdom against kingdom: and there shall be earthquakes in divers places (an 8.1 in Mexico), and there shall be famines (the Sudan) and troubles: these are the beginning of sorrows." - Jesus Christ (Mark 13:8)

"And there shall be signs in the sun and in the moon (coast to coast solar eclipse followed by sun spots unleashing powerful solar flares), and upon the earth distress of nations with perplexity (Brexit and what to do with the numerous refugee influx into Europe); the sea and the waves roaring (hurricanes - Harvey and Irma); - Jesus Christ (Lk 21:25) "The sun shall become so hot that it will scorch men (global warming) and they shall gnaw their tongues for pain and curse the God of heaven that has power over this plague." (The Revelation of Jesus Christ 16:8-10)

"When these things begin to come to pass, look up and lift up your heads for your redemption draweth nigh." Jesus Christ (Lk 21:28) Remember that these are the signs that the Lord Jesus Christ gave of His 2nd Coming or have you forgotten? Churches are not proclaiming this anymore with vigor when you can see these signs of His return on your nightly news broadcast which were once proclaimed in churches. Inform unsuspecting loved ones by sending them a copy or give them the free website to see prophecy in pictures for themselves at www.ProphecyChecklist.com.

James Warden
President of Have You Heard the Good News

"Believe on the Lord Jesus Christ and thou shall be saved." (Acts 16:31)

Free book on line by author at:

HaveYouHeardTheGoodNews.com

One Hundred Reasons Why Born Again Believers Cannot Lose Their Salvation

See Prophecy in Pictures
www.prophecychecklist.com

Prophecy Finder Index:
Your Prophecy Check off Checklist

Section One:
Signs Of The Last Days "The Beginning Of Sorrows"
- ✓ Ground Zero: Israel to become a nation predicted
- ✓ Terrorism toward Israelis predicted
- ✓ Great Earthquakes & Pandemics predicted
- ✓ Fierce Hurricanes and Tsunamis predicted
- ✓ Information Age Prophesied
- ✓ Corporate Greed: The Rich Fraudulently Withholding wages from Laborers in the End Times
- ✓ Successful Gay Rights Movement predicted
- ✓ Jerusalem To Become A Millstone Around The Necks Of Her Allies
- ✓ The Gospel of the Kingdom is Spread Throughout the World
- ✓ The Second Coming of Jesus Christ is to be Mocked As Ridiculous in the Last Days

Section Four:
Global Mass Destruction

✓ One Fourth Of The World's Population is Killed

✓ **The Fourth Horsemen: Widespread Death & Destruction**

✓ Asteroids Spray Earth Causing Dust to Block Sun

✓ A Great Shaking Upon the Earth

✓ The Seventh Seal Opened

✓ Seven Trumpets of Judgment Sound and Earth's Atmosphere Destroys much Plant Life

✓ Asteroid Falls Into the Sea and 1/3 of Sea Life Perishes

✓ One Third of the Earth's Water Supply is Contaminated

✓ Heart Attacks Brought on by Fear

✓ The Skies are Darkened

✓ Oxygen Supply Divinely Protected

✓ New Locust Life Forms Emerge

✓ Iraq Enters World Stage in End Times with 200 Million Man Army Marching Across Her Euphrates Riverbed

✓ Widespread Drug Abuse

Section Five:
The Seven Last Plagues

✓ The Seven Vials of God's Wrath of God Poured on Earth

✓ Much Sea Life Destroyed

✓ Global Warming Peaks

✓ Painful Sores & Darkness Throughout the Earth

✓ Armies Of The East Summoned To Armageddon

✓ The Greatest Earthquake In World History to Occur

✓ Seven Horrors Yet to be Revealed

Section Six:

The Anti-Semite / Antichrist

✓ The Destabilization Of Persia (Iran) by the West

✓ The Anti-Semite / Antichrist Will Not Know He is the Rod of God's Anger

✓ Three Rulers of the Destabilized Middle East Region Will Come to Power Prior to the Rise of the Greatest Anti-Semite Ever, Known as the Antichrist

✓ The First of The Persian Gulf's Last Four Rulers

✓ Second Ruler of Persian Gulf Marries a Princess in a Peace Agreement and Offspring to Wage War

✓ Arabian Rulers Shall War Over Gulf Region

✓ The Second Ruler of Persian Gulf to be Defeated in the Midst of Many Years of Gulf Wars

✓ The Third Gulf Ruler Raises Taxes to Restore Its Infrastructure But Will Die of Natural Causes

✓ The Belief System of the Anti-Semite / Antichrist

✓ The Anti-Semite / Antichrist Honors a Strange God

✓ The Anti-Semite / Antichrist Brings Peace Covenant to the Middle East

✓ Solomon's Temple to be Rebuilt on the Temple Mount

✓ The Assassination of the Anti-Semite / Antichrist

✓ Post-Raptured Pope of Apostate Church Encourages Worship Of the Anti-Semite / Antichrist After His "Resurrection"

✓ Post-Raptured Pope Called, The False Prophet, Commands a Statue be Made for the Anti-Semite/Antichrist After an Assassination Attempt

- ✓ The False Prophet Commands All Nations to Worship the Statue of the Anti-Semite/Antichrist or be Executed
- ✓ The False Prophet Mandates That All Pledge Allegiance to the Anti-Semite/Antichrist by Taking the "Mark"
- ✓ All the Armies of the Earth to Surround Jerusalem and Her Enemies Rejoice
- ✓ Jews Warned to Flee Jerusalem when the Anti-Semite/Antichrist Invades Their Yet-to-Be Rebuilt Jewish temple on the Temple Mount
- ✓ The Anti-Semite/Antichrist Enter the Israelis' Temple Stating He is God
- ✓ The Temple is Defiled by the Anti-Semite / Antichrist
- ✓ The Anti-Semite/Antichrist Curses God Almighty After Declaring Himself to be God
- ✓ The Anti-Semite/Antichrist Curses the Raptured and deceased Saints in Heaven
- ✓ The Anti-Semite/Antichrist Declares War on the Saints of God
- ✓ The Anti-Semite/Antichrist Blasphemes God And Crushes Believers
- ✓ The Anti-Semite/Antichrist Will be Revered
- ✓ The Anti-Semite/Antichrist Goes Forth to Conquer
- ✓ Russia Wars Against the Anti-Semite / Antichrist
- ✓ The Anti-Semite/Antichrist Devastates Egypt
- ✓ The Anti-Semite /Antichrist Enjoys the Spoils of War And Practices Socialism in Redistributing Wealth
- ✓ The Peace Covenant With Israel is Broken
- ✓ Jerusalem is Invaded
- ✓ A Divided Jerusalem to Be Plundered

- ✓ Jerusalem under Siege by the Anti-Semite / Antichrist Man-Made Famine Spawns Cannibalism
- ✓ Two-thirds of Jews Massacred by the Anti-Semite / Antichrist, as Israel Looks in Vain For America to Rescue Her; Only One-Third of the Jewish Population in the Land of Israel will Survive
- ✓ The World is Astonished at the Invasion of Israel and the Siege of Jerusalem
- ✓ The Anti-Semite/Antichrist is Called a Destroyer of the Gentiles [A Term for Europeans in Scripture]
- ✓ 144,000 Jewish Men Ordained by God to Preach the Gospel of the Kingdom During the Tribulation
- ✓ The Gospel of the Kingdom is Preached to All The World then Shall the End Come
- ✓ God Commissions Two Witnesses to Earth
- ✓ Worldwide Media Covers the Deaths of the Two Witnesses
- ✓ Believers Will Be Betrayed to the State by Family Members
- ✓ The Anti-Semite/Antichrist Will Behead Preachers of the Gospel of Christ's Return, the Gospel of the Kingdom
- ✓ The Anti-Semite/Antichrist Makes War Against God's Saints
- ✓ God Avenges His Martyred Saints
- ✓ Martyred Saints Receive White Robes from God
- ✓ Post-Raptured Catholic Church of Rome is Judged
- ✓ The Anti-Semite / Antichrist Attacks Vatican City
- ✓ The Stage is Set for the Great Battle of Armageddon

Section Seven:
The Coming Of The Lord
- ✓ The Lord Assembles His Mighty Army to Invade Earth

- ✓ Jesus Christ Returns
- ✓ The Second Coming of Jesus Christ
- ✓ The Earth Laments Christ's Return
- ✓ All Tribes of the Earth Mourn Christ's Return
- ✓ Every Eye on Earth Shall See His Second Coming
- ✓ Kings of the Earth Make War Against Christ at His Return
- ✓ The Lord Takes Vengeance on Unbelievers
- ✓ The Battle of Armageddon, Christ Massacres Earth's Armies
- ✓ The Lord Will Fight for Jerusalem
- ✓ The Lord Destroys Those Who Fought Against Jerusalem
- ✓ The Lord Utters His Mighty Voice Before His Army and His Saints Execute Judgment
- ✓ Jesus Christ Smites the Nations
- ✓ Christ Slays the Armies Gathered at Armageddon
- ✓ The Blood of The 200 Million Man Armies, Slain by Christ at Armageddon, Will Be More Than Three Feet Deep and Cover Over 100 Miles
- ✓ Christ Puts Down The Anti-Semite / Antichrist & Waters the Battlefield with the Blood of Earth's Armies
- ✓ The Anti-Semite / Antichrist's Power is Broken

Section Eight:
The Day OF THE Lord
- ✓ The Kings of the Earth are Punished
- ✓ The Day of the Lord
- ✓ Christ Reveals the Wounds From His Crucifixion to the Jewish Survivors of the Anti-Semite / Antichrist Siege
- ✓ Jewish Survivors of the Tribulation Mourn the Sins of Their Forefathers' Crucifixion of Jesus Christ

Section Nine:
Christ's Millennial Reign

✓ The Millennial (Thousand Year) Reign of Jesus Christ Begins

✓ Satan is Bound for a Thousand Years and Cast into the Bottomless Pit

✓ Satan Mocked by World Leaders Already in Hell as he Descends into Its Pit

✓ Christ Establishes Jerusalem as the Capitol of the World

✓ Jerusalem Finally at Peace

✓ The House of the Lord Shall Be Established

✓ Christ Brings True Peace to the Middle East

✓ A Highway Out of Egypt is to be Built

✓ Peace on Earth The Lion Will Lie Down in Peace with the Lamb

✓ Israel to be Comforted by Her King

✓ Jesus Christ Reigns in Jerusalem as King of Kings and Lord of Lords

✓ The Original Twelve Apostles Are Installed as Judges Over Israel

✓ Christ Annexes Vast Amounts of Land in the Mid-East as New Israel to Fulfill God's Old Testament Promise to, His Chosen People, The Jews

✓ All Nations to Send Delegates Annually to the Feast of Tabernacles or be Punished

✓ A Coup Will Take Place Against Christ's Rule

✓ The Deceiver To Be Cast Into the Lake of Fire

✓ Christ Holds Court

✓ The Great White Throne: Judgment Day

- ✓ Jesus Christ Abdicates Earthly Throne in Jerusalem to Install David as King of Jerusalem as Promised
- ✓ The Day of the Lord Comes as a Thief in the Night followed by the day of God
- ✓ Lifespan of Earth's Inhabitants Increased
- ✓ Christ Restores Heaven & Earth Back to His Father as Perfect and the Last Enemy Death is Destroyed
- ✓ Christ Reigns as King of Kings from New Jerusalem
- ✓ God's Plan for Ages to Come

Section Ten:
Signs of His Second Coming
- ✓ Warning Signs Of His Second Coming A Party Atmosphere Prevails Prior to the Lord's Return
- ✓ Church Leaders Departing From the Faith
- ✓ Widespread Backsliding Becomes Commonplace in the Church
- ✓ Many Will Claim to be Christ
- ✓ A Perfect Convergence of All Signs to Manifest in One Generation
- ✓ Perilous Times Shall Come
- ✓ No Man Knows the Day or the Hour of Christ's Return
- ✓ Signs of the Times
- ✓ Because crime shall abound The Love of Many Shall Wax Cold
- ✓ He Will Return Quickly
- ✓ Watch!
- ✓ How To Escape The Wrath To Come
- ✓ The Rapture of the Church Will Take Place Before the Great Tribulation Strikes Earth

- ✓ After the Rapture, All Believers Must Appear Before the Judgment Seat of Christ
- ✓ The Marriage Supper
- ✓ Bridal feast
- ✓ Christ Will Receive Those He Redeemed To Himself
- ✓ The Last Words of Jesus Christ in the Book of the Revelation
- ✓ The Time is at Hand…

Section Eleven:
The Biblical History of Iraq

Section Twelve:
The Prophetic Fulfillment of God's Timetable Through Jewish Feast
- ✓ Feast Of Passover
- ✓ Feast Of Unleavened Bread
- ✓ Feast Of First Fruits
- ✓ Feast Of Pentecost
- ✓ Feast Of Trumpets
- ✓ Day Of Atonement ✓ Feast Of Tabernacles

Free Book Online

When you believe in Jesus Christ for eternal salvation your faith has been exchanged for His eternal righteousness. For more information on the permanence of your eternal salvation another FREE BOOK ONE HUNDRED REASONS WHY BORN AGAIN BELIEVERS CANNOT LOSE THEIR SALVATION is online at:

www.haveyouheardthegoodnews.com

For a copy of this book as an e-book to read on your phone or to order it in paperback go to: www.prophecychecklist.com.

Biography

James Warden is an ordained minister and has been a Christian Contemporary music radio announcer. he founded Have You Heard the Good News in 1992; a ministry dedicated to the proclamation and teaching of salvation by grace through faith. After repeated trips to Nigeria, Ghana, Benin, Kenya, and Ethiopia to train ministers in Africa, he resigned a pastorate to devote himself to complete a Master's of Theology at Dallas Theological Seminary in Texas where he resides with his wife. His seminary training inspired him to develop an online African Bible College (ABC) to educate its ministers in Soteriology - The Doctrine of Salvation, Eschatology - Bible Prophecy, and Blacks in Bible history. He serves on the board of Repairer of the Breach ministries and has written two other books *Prophecy Checklist: Over One Hundred Jewish Prophecies Describing the End Times*, and *One Hundred Reasons Why Born Again Believers Cannot Lose Their Salvation*, and *The Complete Works of Blacks in the Bible*. Pastor Warden serves at Our Calling Shelter in Dallas, Texas and may be contacted by e-mail at ministrymailnews@aol.com.